To the children of Carlton Primary School, London NW5,
who have taught me about recorder teaching since 1974.

# me and my recorder
## part 1

Marlene Hobsbawm

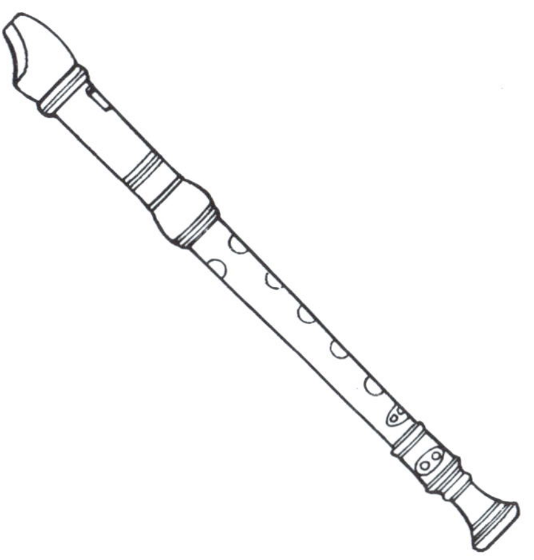

© 1989 by Marlene Hobsbawm
First published in 1989 by Faber Music Ltd
Bloomsbury House 74–77 Great Russell Street London WC1B 3DA
Designed and illustrated by Julia Osorno
Music drawn by Sheila Stanton
Typeset by Bookworm Typesetting Manchester
Printed in England by Caligraving Ltd
All rights reserved

ISBN10: 0-571-51045-0
EAN13: 978-0-571-51045-0

To buy Faber Music publications or to find out about the full range of titles available
please contact your local music retailer or Faber Music sales enquiries:

Faber Music Limited, Burnt Mill, Elizabeth Way, Harlow, CM20 2HX England
Tel: +44 (0)1279 82 89 82   Fax: +44 (0)1279 82 89 83
sales@fabermusic.com   fabermusic.com

# For Teachers and Parents

**Me and My Recorder** (parts 1 and 2) is for children to use in school and at home. While I have assumed that children using these books will learn with teachers, the material is presented so that they can also use it by themselves once the class is over. The aim is to enable children to understand and remember what they are doing step by step.

I hope the books will provide a sound foundation for learning to read music. The descant recorder is often the first musical instrument children learn, and this is, therefore, the time when their curiosity and interest in the new language of music is greatest. It is important not to let that moment pass.

In working with children I have found that one of the most effective ways of beginning the descant recorder is to play four notes – either A, G, E, B *or* B, A, G, E – before introducing staff notation. Children want to start playing the new instrument straight away. Their interest can be centred on producing the sounds, listening to them and playing them in a variety of musical ways. It is often after this initial skill has been acquired that it becomes fun to learn to read music.

Parts 1 and 2 together cover the beginnings of recorder playing and music making. So many school recorder teachers have told me they would welcome a method that moves at a realistic pace and provides them with several tunes to play before new information is added. The books have been written with this in mind.

While **Me and My Recorder** is aimed primarily at children, this system of learning the recorder has also been found very useful with older beginners.

**Marlene Hobsbawm**
London, 1989

# For American Readers

In this book, English note-values are used rather than their U.S. equivalents:

| **English** | **U.S.** |
| --- | --- |
| Semibreve | Whole note |
| Minim | Half note |
| Crotchet | Quarter note |
| Quaver | Eighth note |

The term 'note' is used to identify pitches ('tone' in U.S. usage) as well as their symbolic representations.

# Acknowledgements

Nobody writes such a book entirely alone, and I have consulted and been helped by many friends in the world of music education, and especially by my friends in The Society of Recorder Players.

But there are three people who have been much more closely involved in the preparation of these recorder books, and whose help has really been essential: Diane Jamieson (*Primrose Hill Infants School*), Angela Mendis (*Fleet Primary School*) and Pat Wrench (*Edward Wilson School*).

I would also like to thank Indrani Sen.

# The Descant Recorder



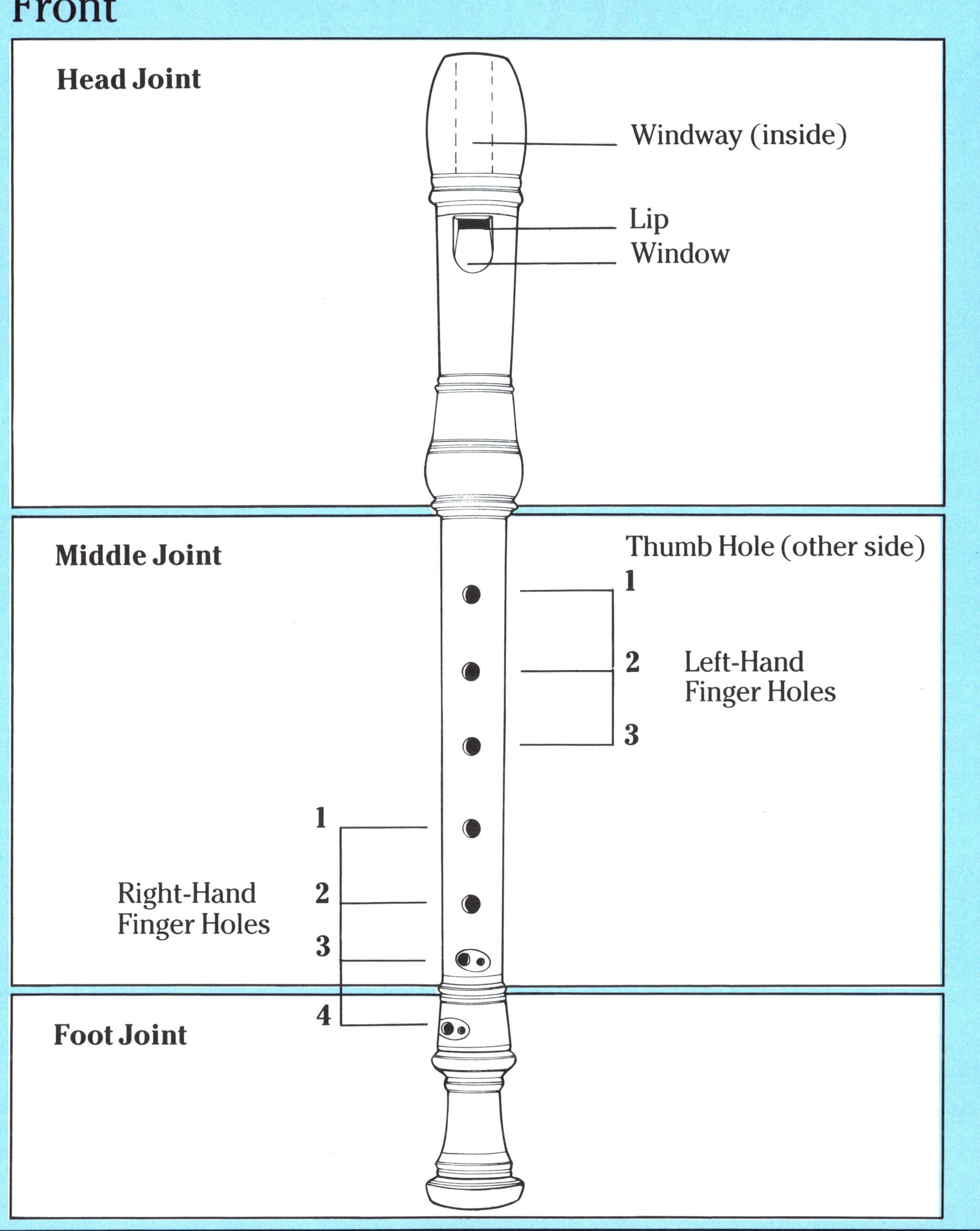

# How to hold your Recorder

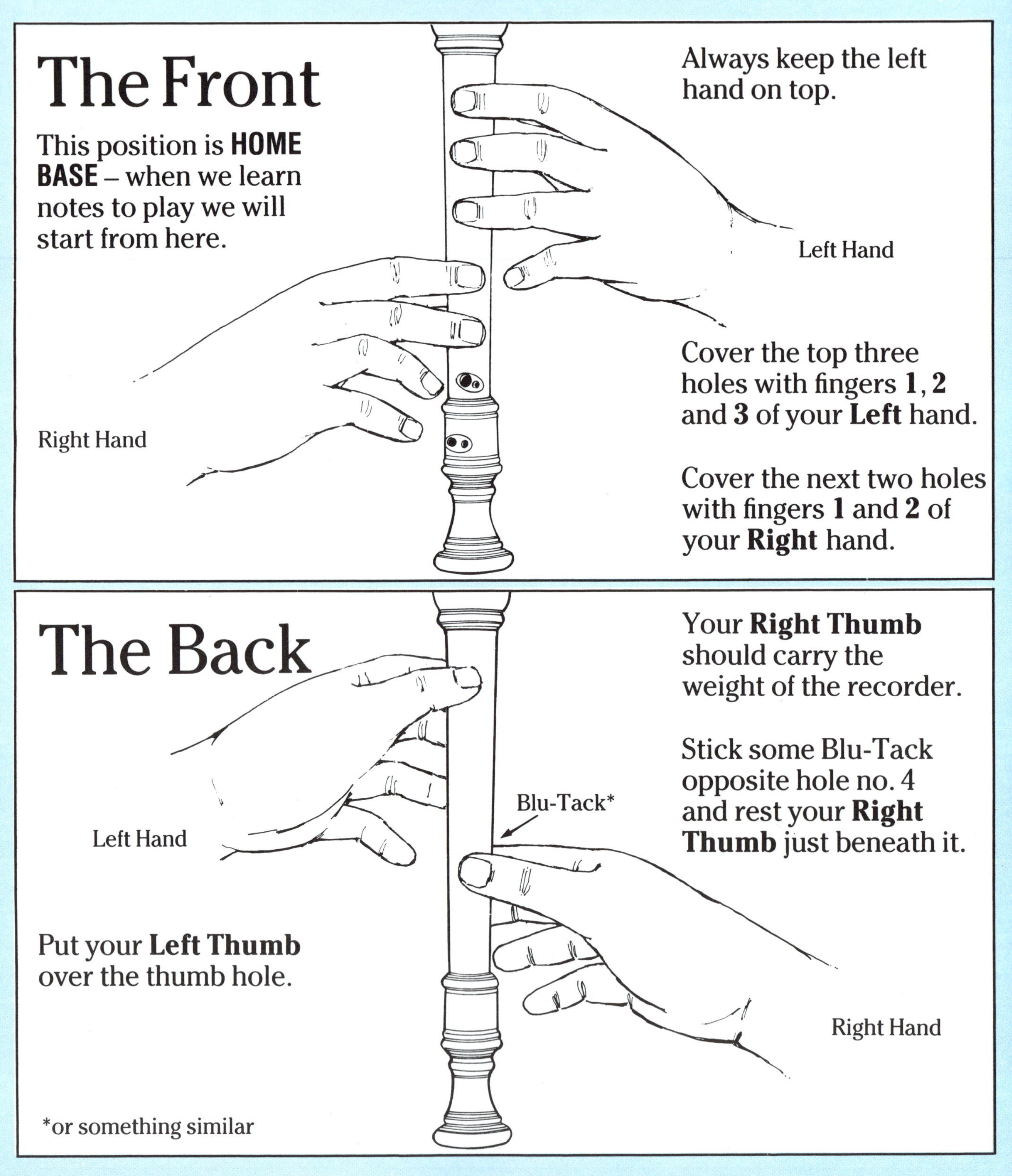

# Look at your Left Palm

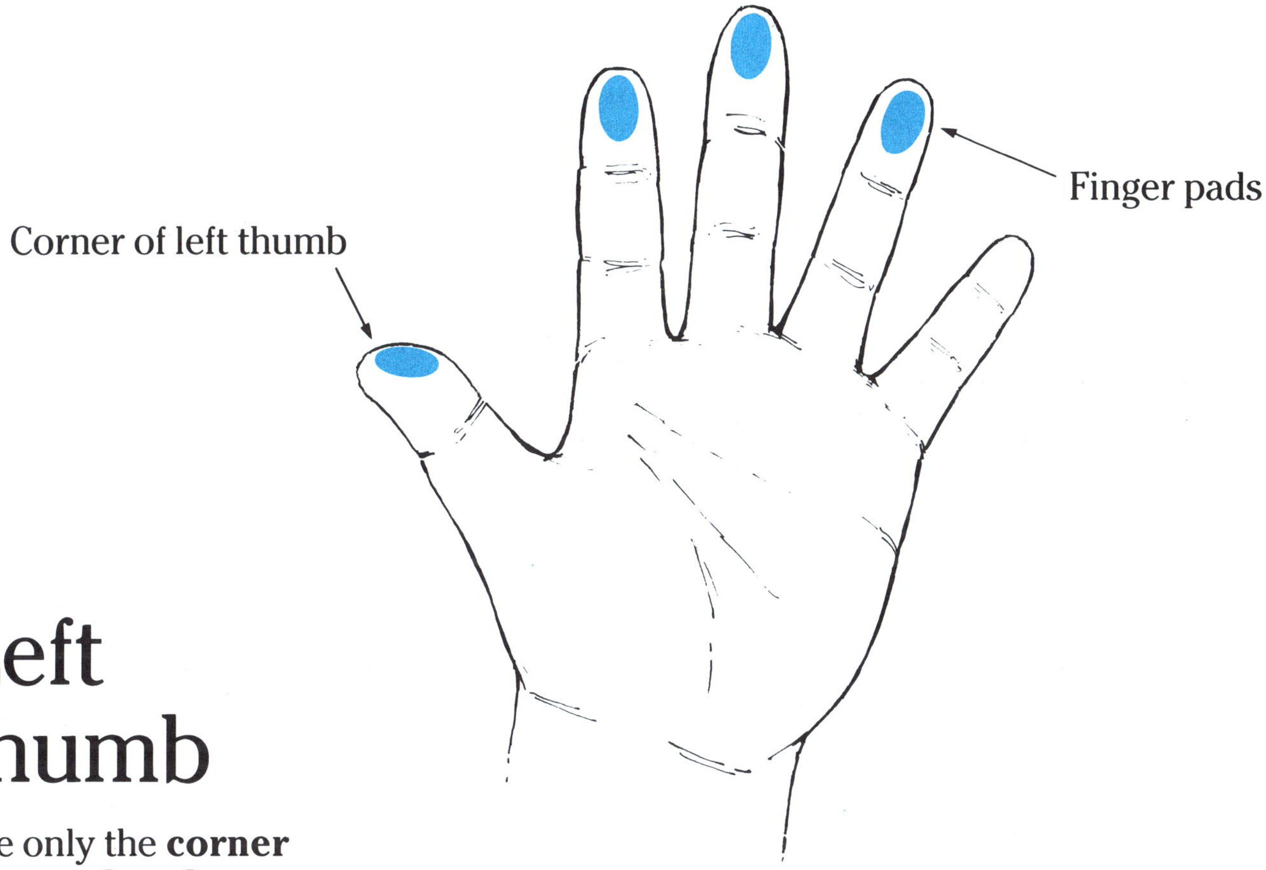

Corner of left thumb

Finger pads

## Left thumb

Use only the **corner of your thumb** to cover the thumb-hole at the back.

## Fingers

Use only the **pads of your fingers** to cover the holes on the front.

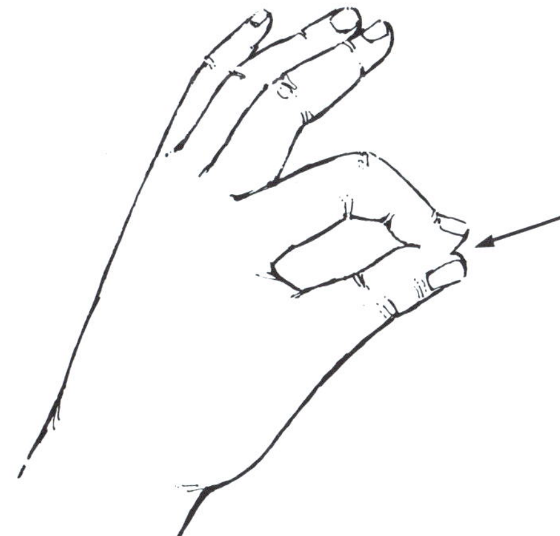

Make this shape to find the corner of your thumb.

Your fingers should be **Flat** not curved.

# A

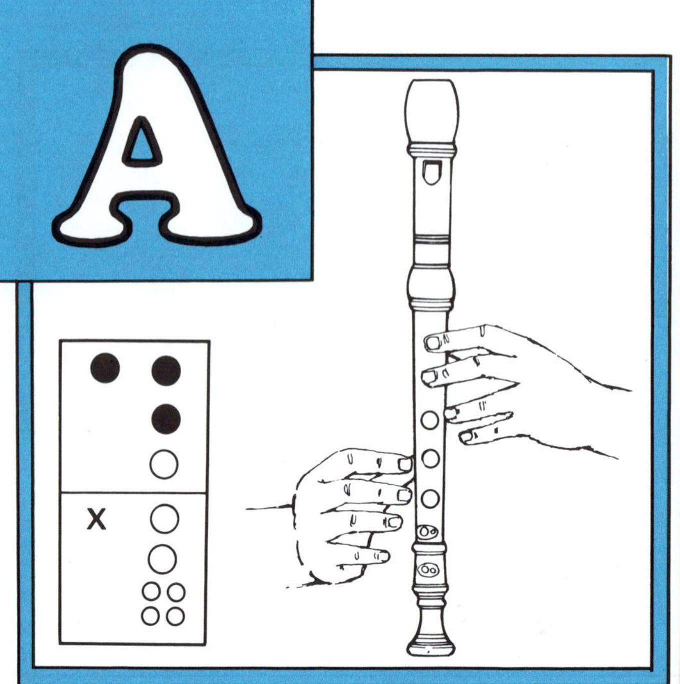

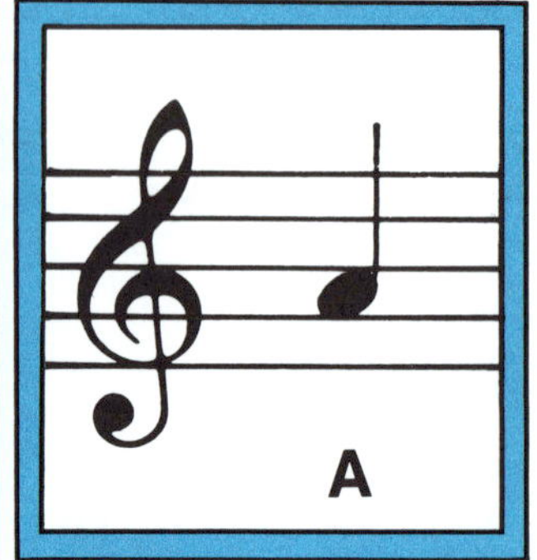



## Our first note is **A**.

Start from **HOME BASE**. Slightly lift up all the fingers, leaving on left-hand fingers 1 and 2.

# Tonguing

Tonguing means using your **Tongue** to whisper into your recorder. Whisper 'Doo Doo Doo'.

**SAY AND PLAY**

**1.**

Now let's play.
**A** **A** **A**
Doo Doo Doo

**2.**

Have a nice day.
**A** **A** **A** **A**
Doo Doo Doo Doo

Always blow into your recorder **Gently**.

## SAY AND PLAY

**3.**

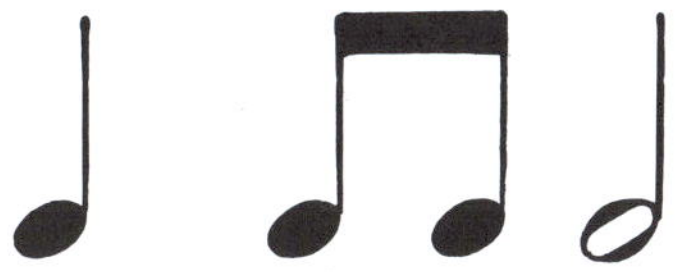

Knock at the door.
**A A A A**

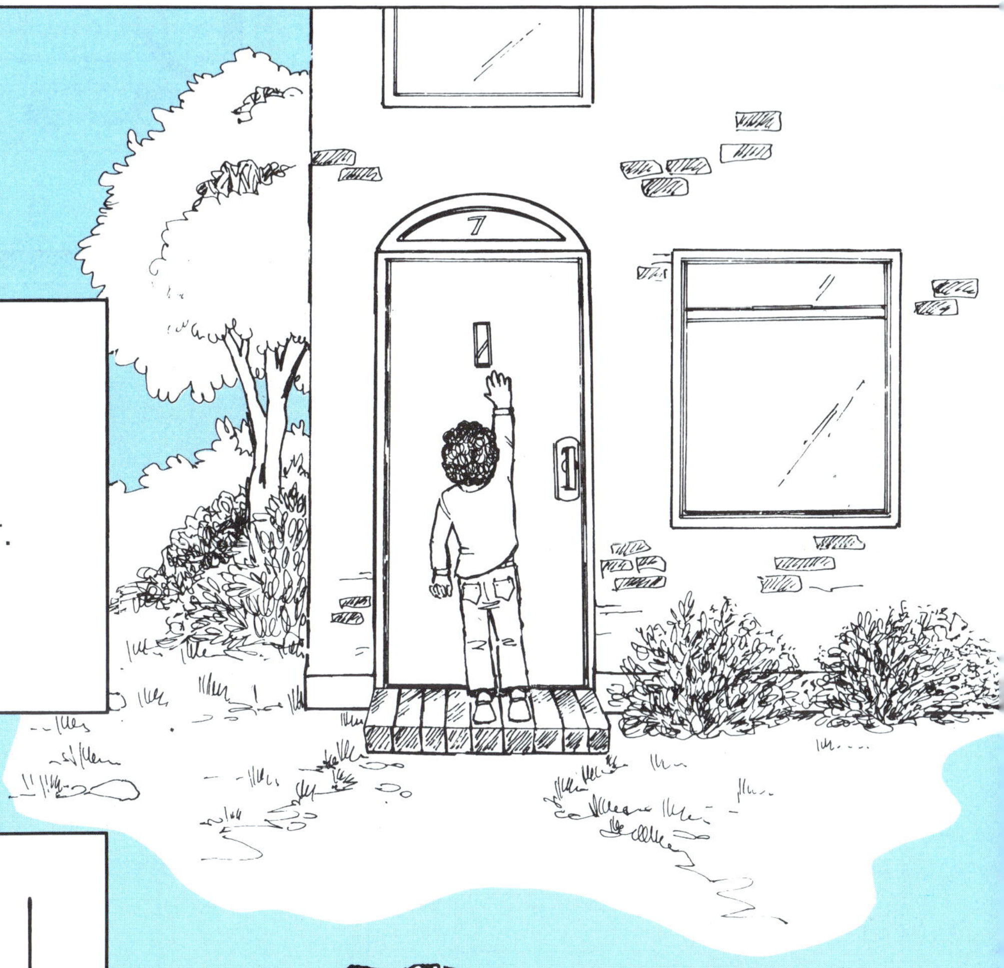

**4.**

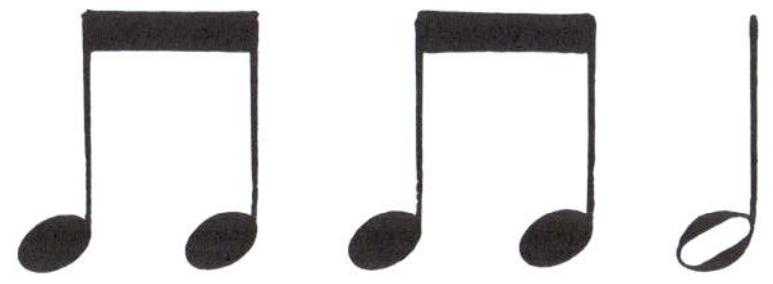

Give a dog a bone.
**A A A A A**

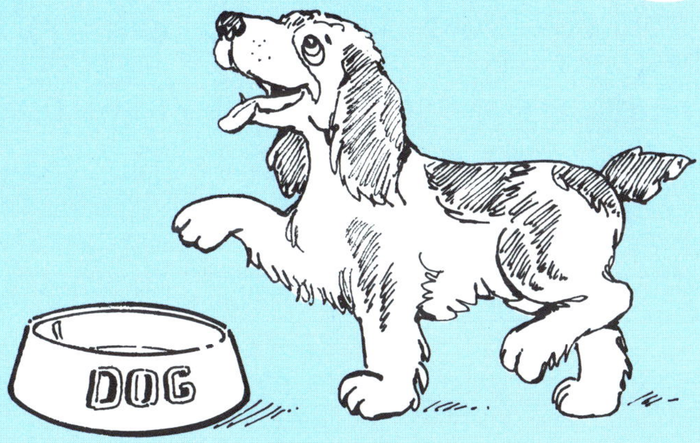

If your recorder sounds blocked up, put a finger across the **'window'** of the recorder and blow firmly.

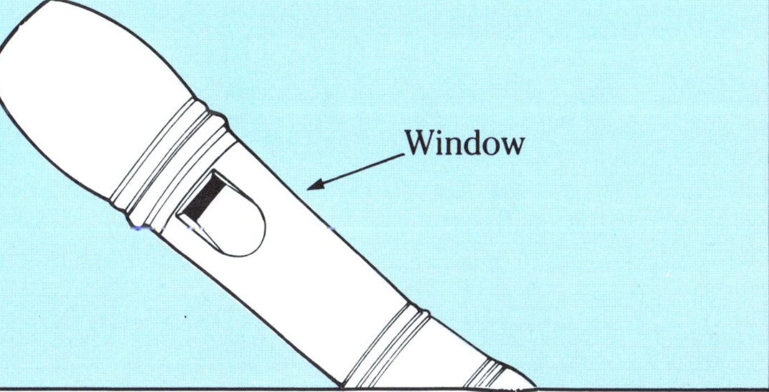

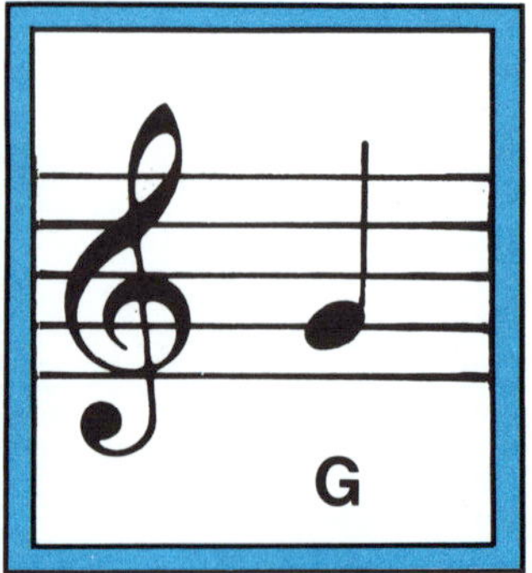

# G

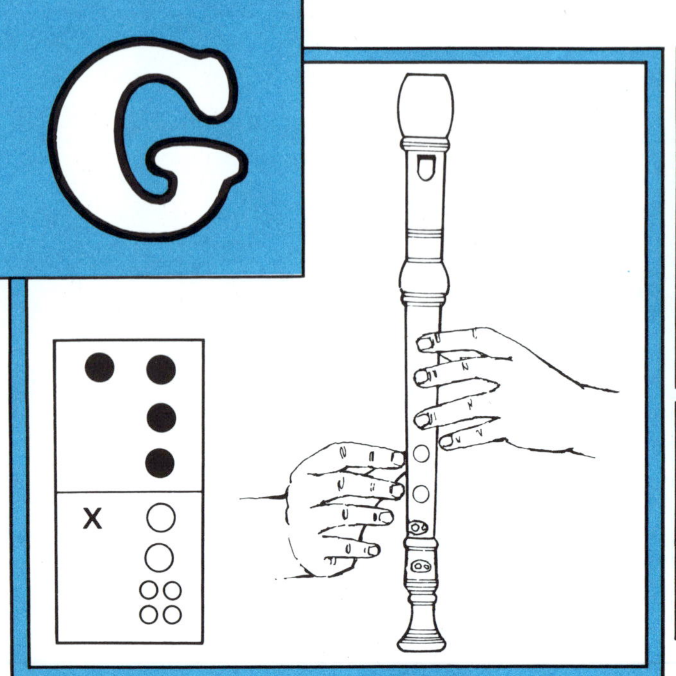

## Our next note is **G**.

Start from **HOME BASE**. Then slightly lift up the right-hand fingers.

### SAY AND PLAY

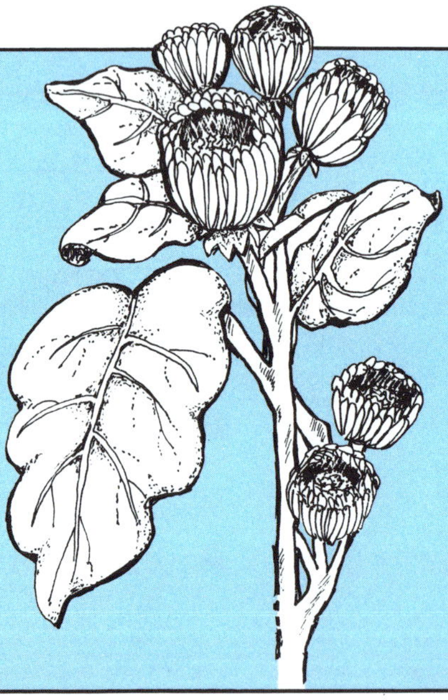

**1.**

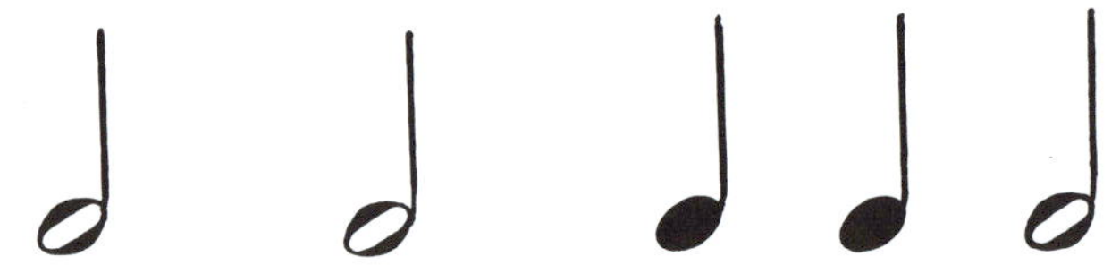

East. West. Mum knows best.

**G G G G G**

**2.**

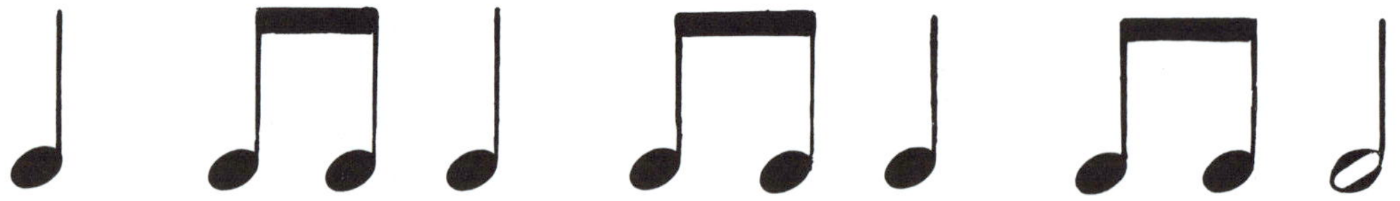

Two fin - gers Three fin - gers Two fin - gers Three.

**A A A G G G A A A G**

Remember to play with your fingers **Flat**.

Make up your own **SAY AND PLAY**.

# E

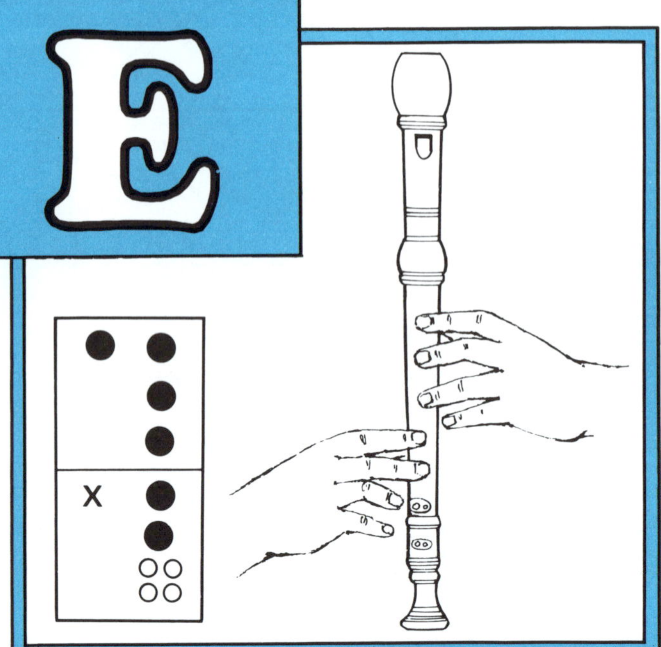

## Our next note is **E**.

**E** is **HOME BASE**. Blow this low note very gently.



Now you know three notes, you can make lots of different patterns with them. Here are three patterns; play each box carefully many times. Now make up your own patterns.

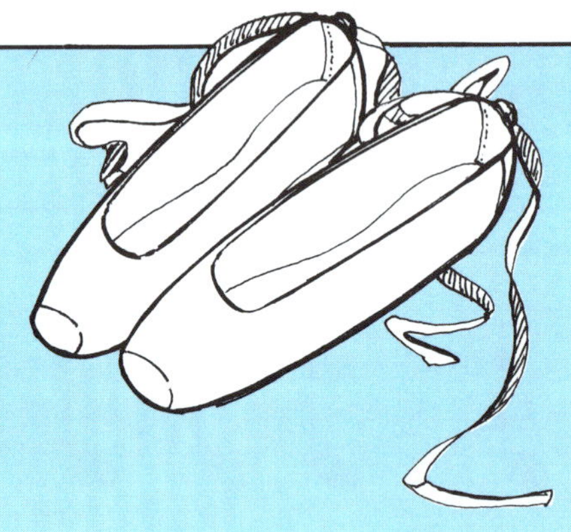

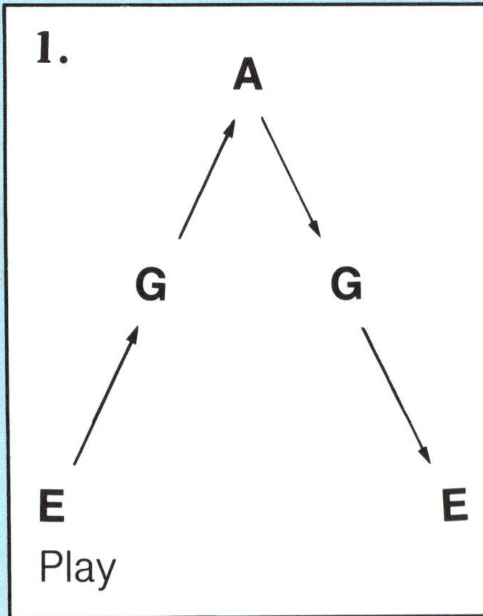


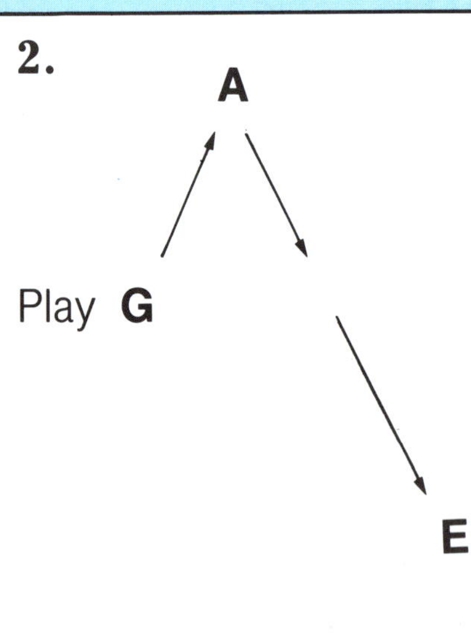


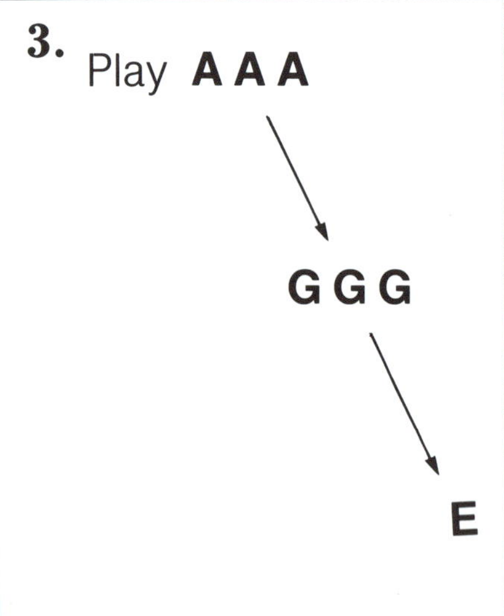


**Cover the full circles of the holes with your finger pads.**
Make sure you don't leave any spaces for leaks.

SAY AND PLAY

1.
Lis - ten to the waves.
E E E E E

2.
Yo - o heave ho Yo - o heave ho!
G E A E G E A E

3.
Fare - well, cliffs of Do - ver.
A A G G E E

# B

X

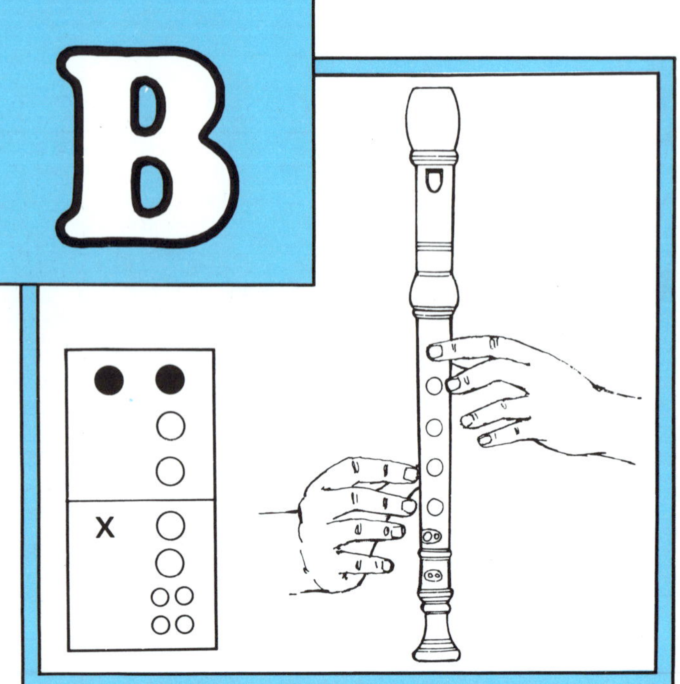

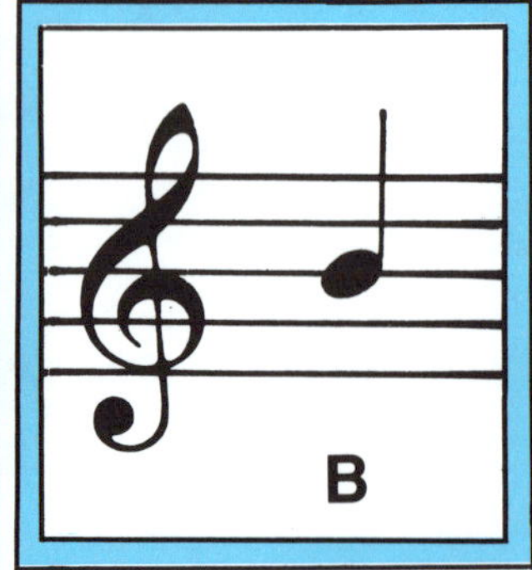

B

## Our next note is **B**.

Start from **E (HOME BASE)**. Slightly lift up all the fingers except left finger 1.

## PRACTICE PATTERNS

1.
Play
B B B
A A A
G G G
E

2.
Play
B
B
B
G
G

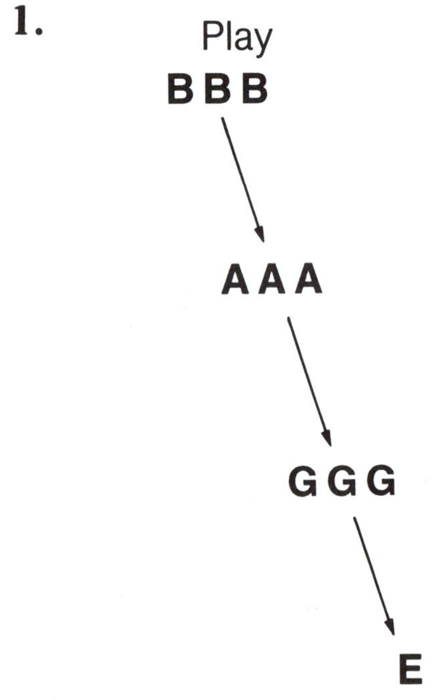

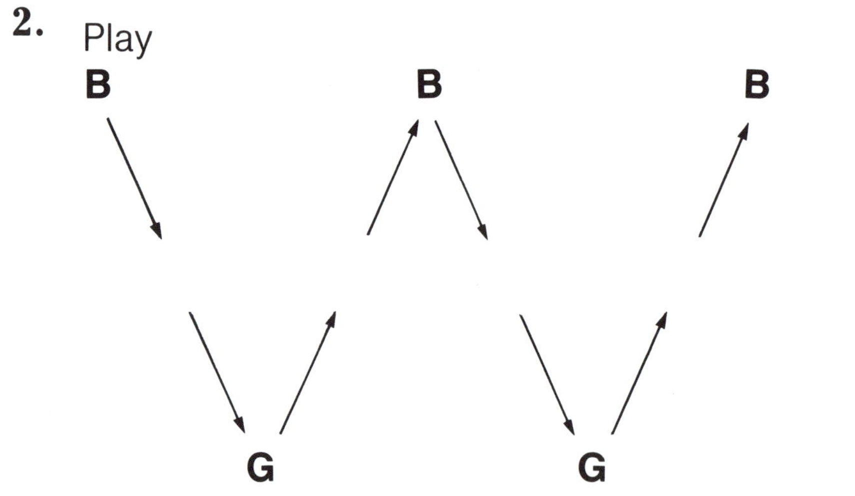

Your **Left** fingers 2 and 3 must move together neatly in this pattern.

Always remember to support the recorder with your right thumb.

**1.**

Sleep   ba - by sleep,
**B**   **A**   **A**   **G**

Fa - ther minds the sheep.
**B**   **B**   **A**   **A**   **G**

**2.**

Leaves   are   fal - ling,   soft   and   gent - le.
**B**   **B**   **B**   **G**   **B**   **B**   **B**   **G**

Sum - mer's   gone,
**A**   **A**   **A**

Au - tumn's   here.
**B**   **A**   **G**

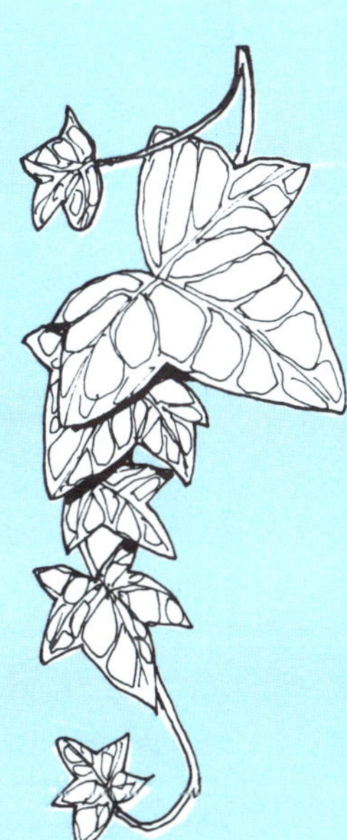

# Reading Notes for the Descant Recorder

We write notes on a **STAVE**.

A **STAVE** has **five lines** and **four spaces**.

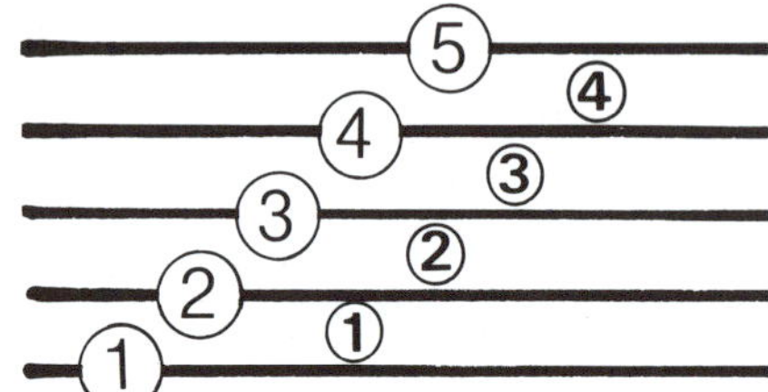

Some **NOTES** have a line through the middle.

Some **NOTES** sit in a space.

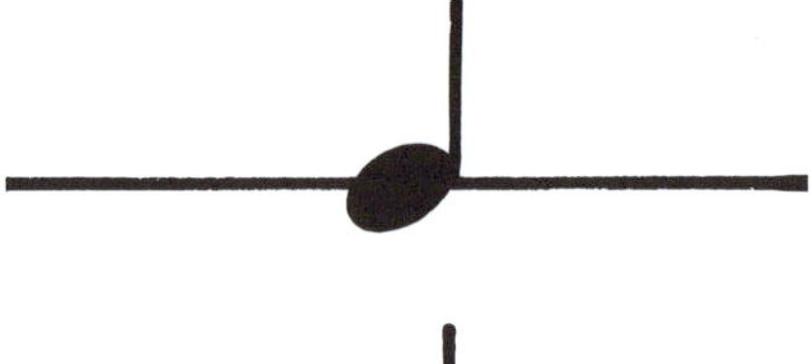

We write a sign at the beginning called a **TREBLE CLEF**.

Here are four notes to learn and draw:

# Timing

## Beat

Music has a steady **BEAT**, like the tick of a clock.

Tick   Tock   Tick   Tock
/     /     /     /

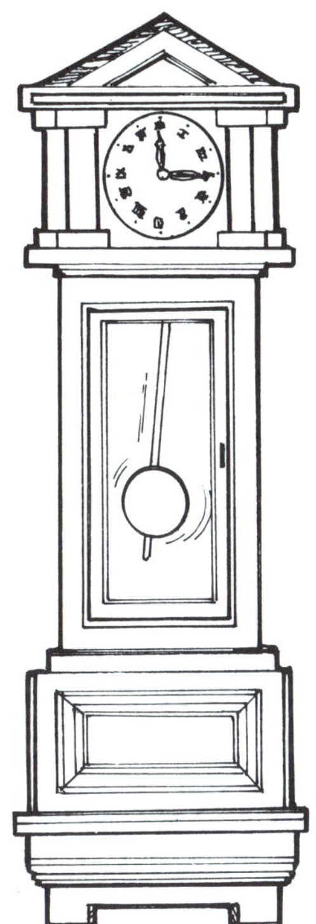

These **SHAPES** tell us to play our sounds **Long** or **Short**:

**Minim**

**Crotchet**

**A pair of Quavers**

# Crotchet

We are going to count a **CROTCHET** as **One** steady beat.

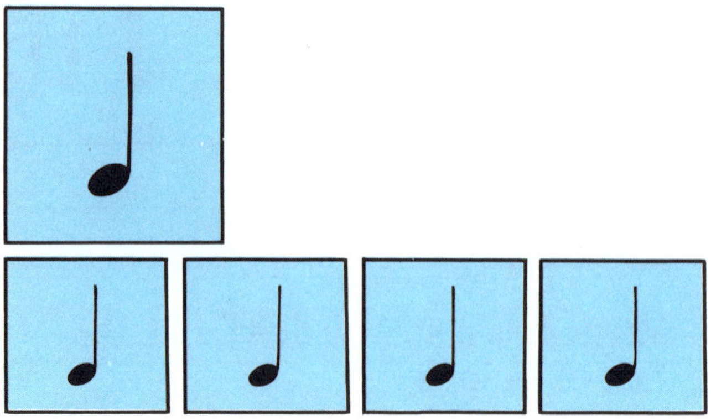

Tick    Tock    Tick    Tock
/     /     /     /

**PLAYBOXES**

Play each box many times.

1.
B   B   B   B
/   /   /   /

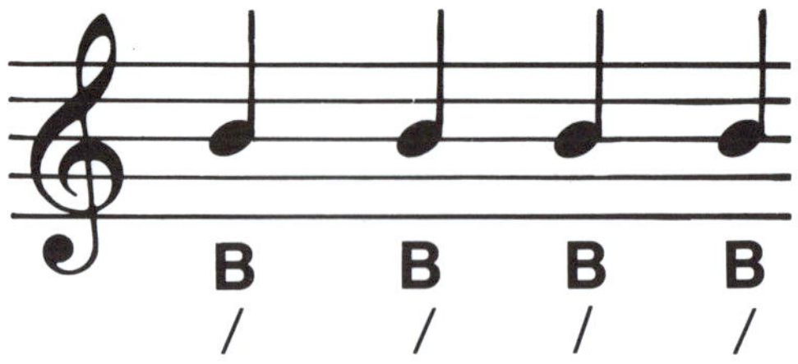

2.
B   A   G   E
/   /   /   /

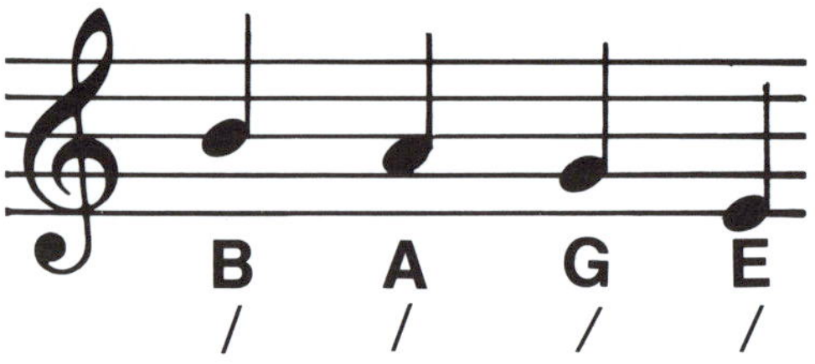

# Minim

We count a **MINIM** as **Two** steady beats.

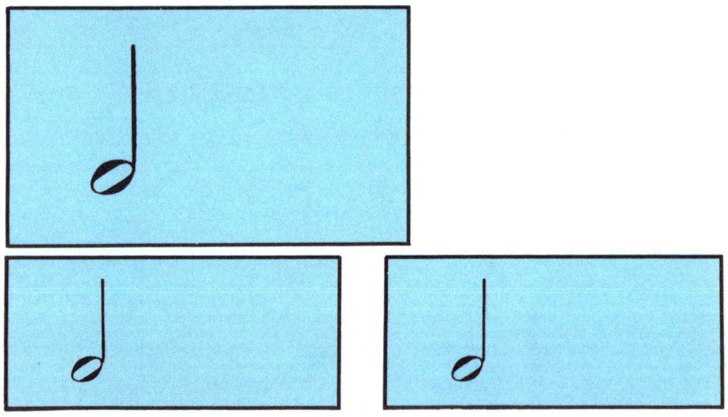

Tick Tock      Tick Tock
/   /      /   /

**PLAYBOXES**

Play each box many times.

1.
A   G
/ /   / /

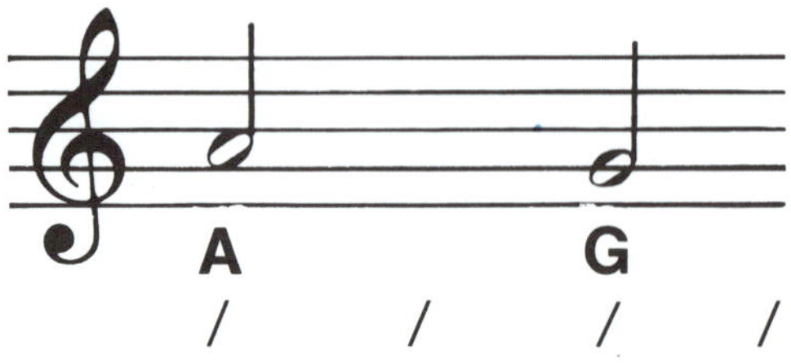

2.
A   A   G
/   /   / /

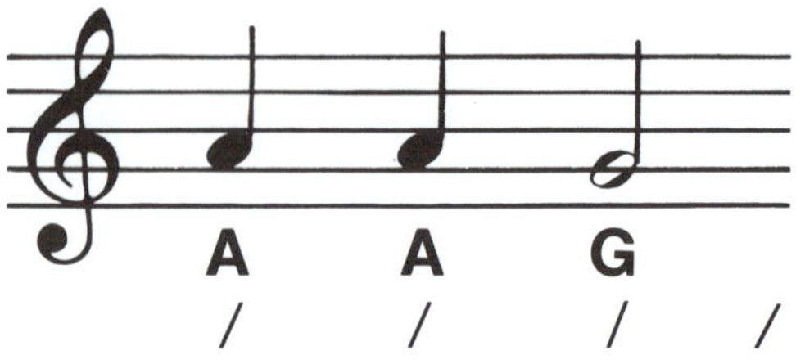

# Quavers

Two **QUAVERS** together make **One** beat.

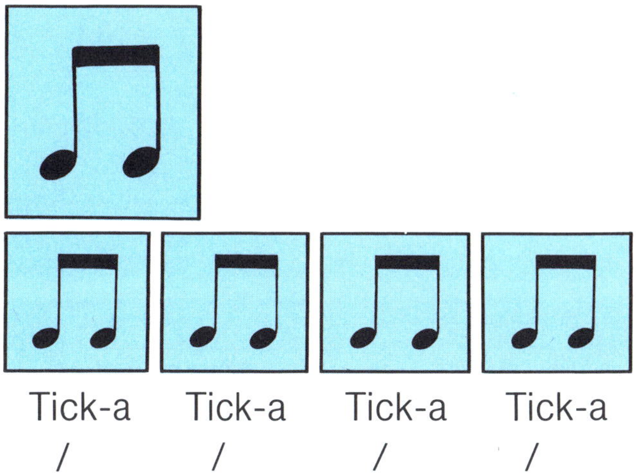

Tick-a / Tick-a / Tick-a / Tick-a /


**PLAYLINES**

1.

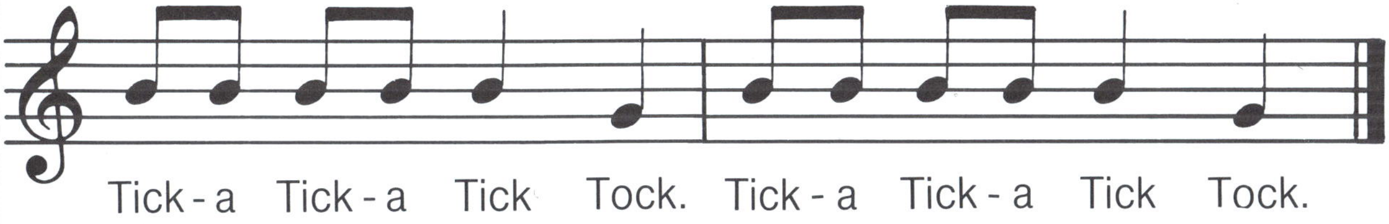

Tick - a Tick - a Tick Tock. Tick - a Tick - a Tick Tock.


2.

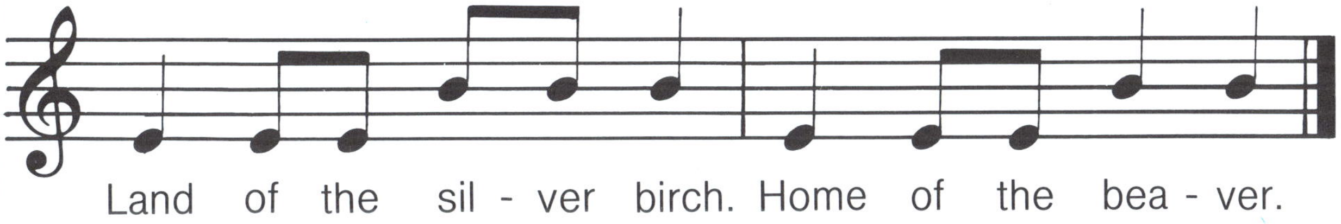

Land of the sil - ver birch. Home of the bea - ver.


# Bars

Music is divided up evenly into **BARS**. To show where the bars are, we put in **BAR LINES**, like this:

To show that the music is finished, we put two lines called a **DOUBLE BAR**, like this:

**1.**

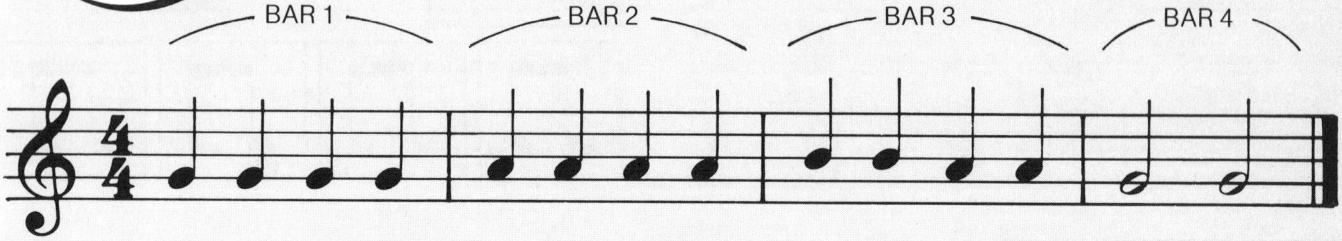

**2.**

**3.**

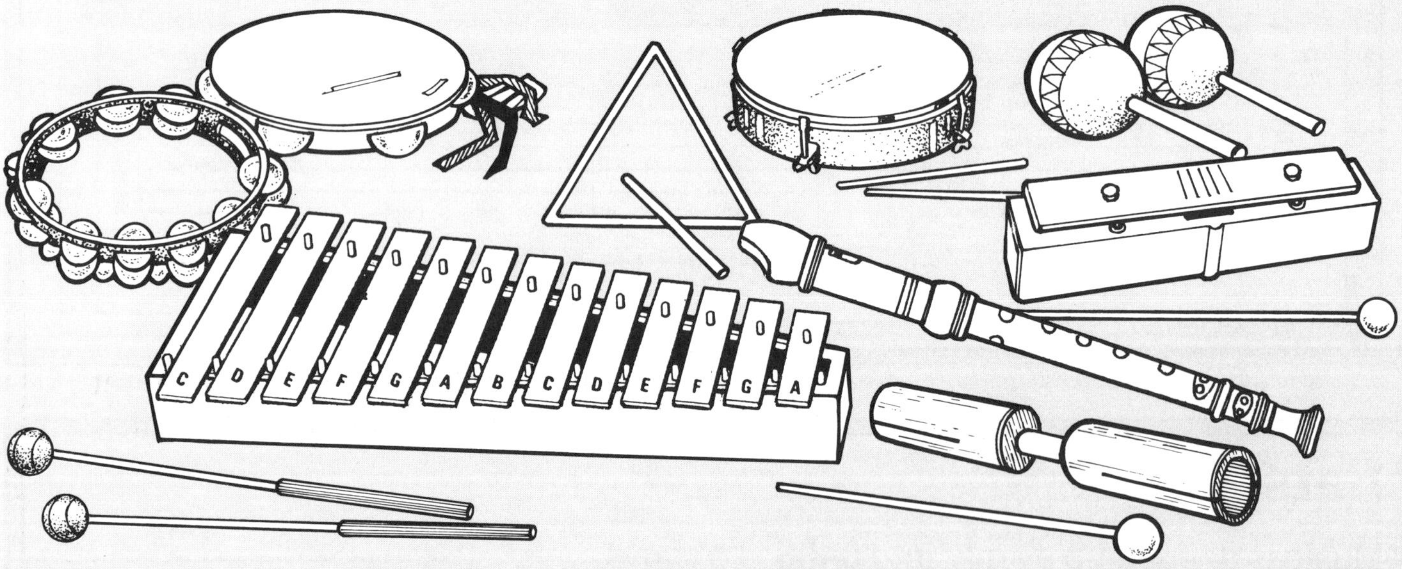

$\frac{4}{4}$ is the same as **C** It means there are **Four** crotchet beats ( / / / / ) in every bar of music.

1.

2.

3.

$\frac{2}{4}$ is the same as **2** over a crotchet

It means there are **Two** crotchet beats (/ /) in every bar of music.

## Time Signatures

These signs $\frac{4}{4}$ $\frac{2}{4}$ are called **TIME SIGNATURES**.

# Tunes to Play

The letters over the notes are **CHORD SYMBOLS** for **piano** or **guitar** accompaniment.

# Light the Candle

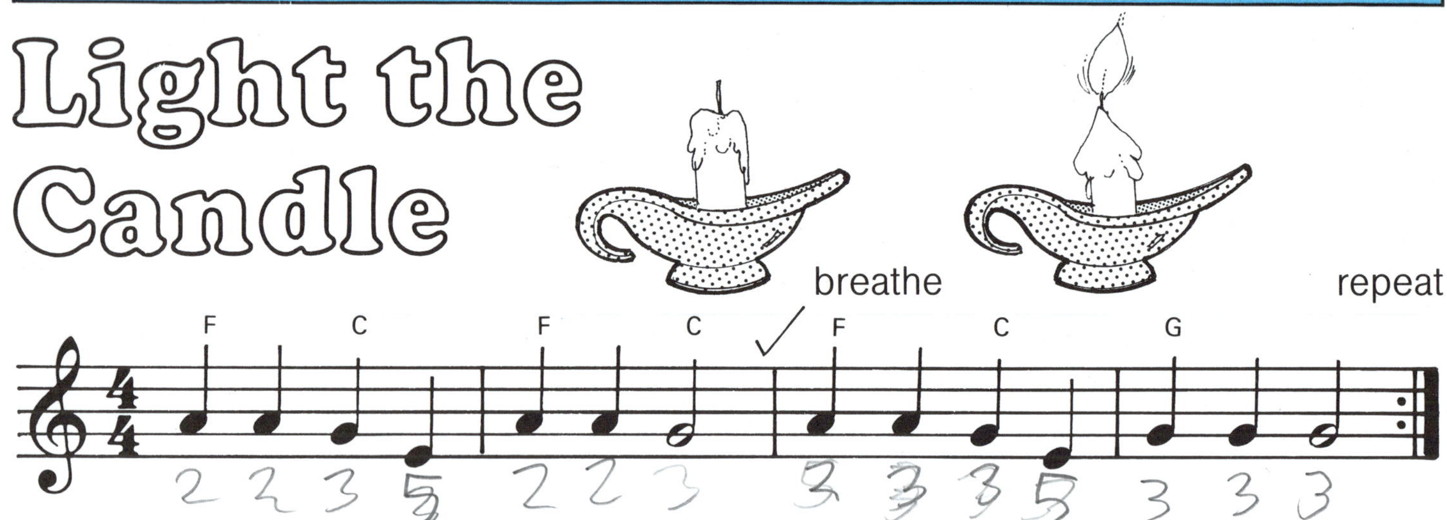




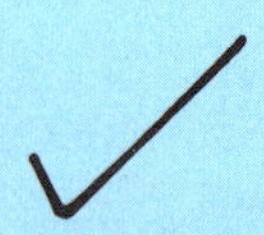 This is a **BREATH MARK**. It means take a breath here.

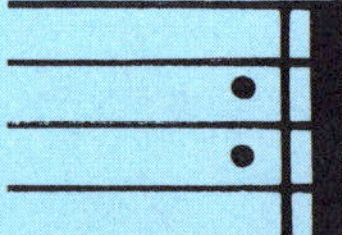 This is a **REPEAT SIGN**. It means play the music through one more time.

# Mary had a Little Lamb



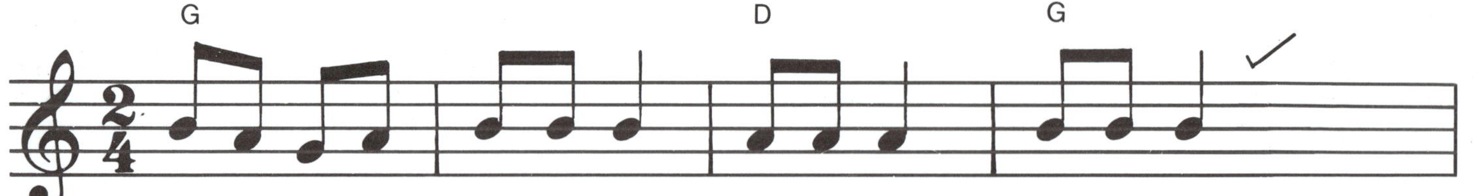

# Copycat Song

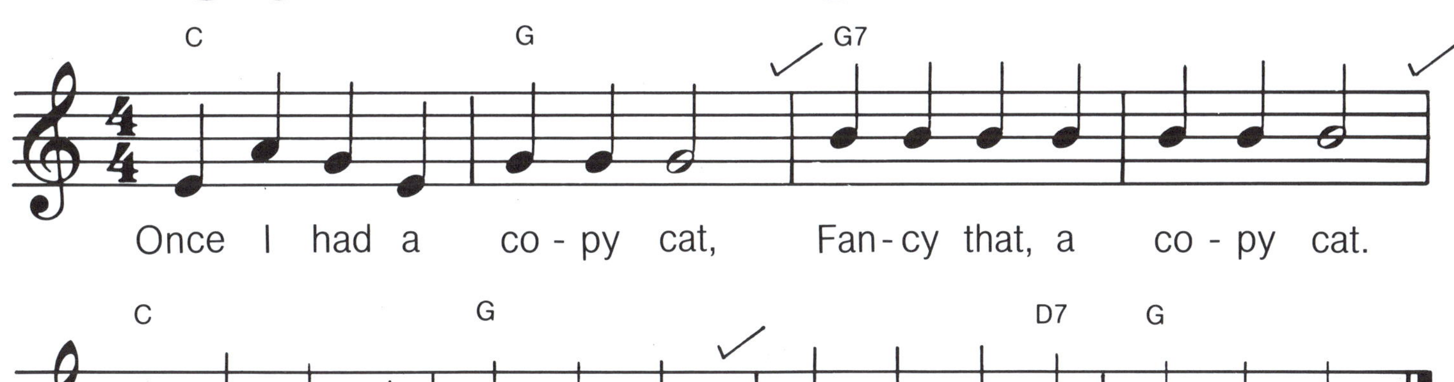

# Boatman's Song

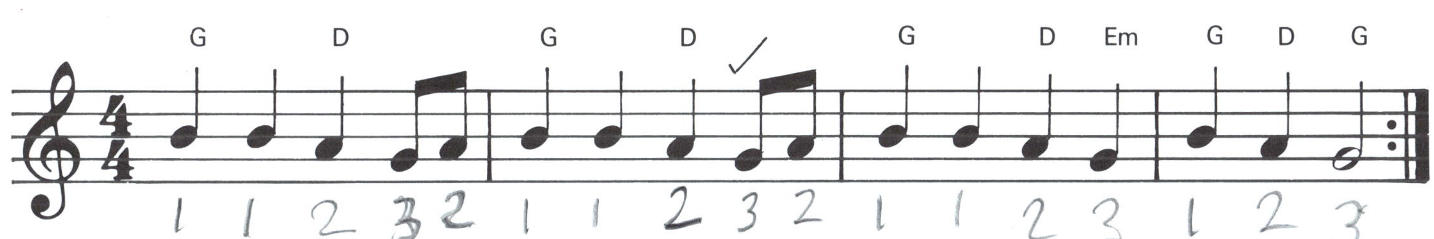


## More on Tonguing

When you whisper 'Doo Doo Doo', feel your tongue move forwards to touch your top teeth, and then back again.

# Chinese Bells

# Trotting

# This Is How Your Body Should Be

### Head

Hold your head up straight.

### Shoulders

Keep your shoulders low.

### Chest

Make your chest feel as **wide** as possible.

### Waistband

Breathe in deeply. Fill your waistband with air.

### Back

Sit with a straight back at the front of your chair.

### Mouth and Lips

Your mouth and lips should be loose and relaxed.

### Wrists

Your wrists should be as straight as possible.

# Semibreve

This is a **SEMIBREVE**. It's held for **Four** steady beats.

# Falling Leaves

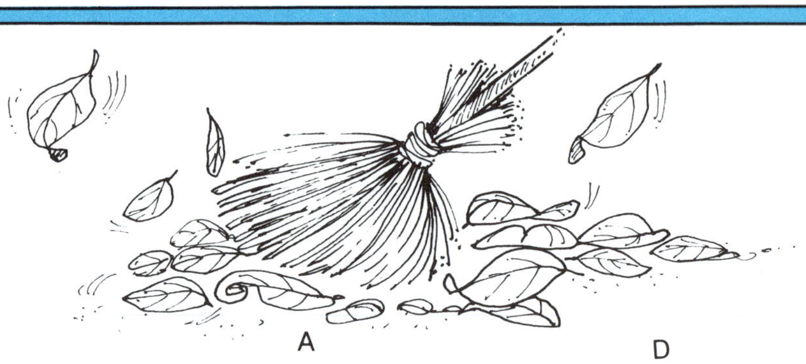

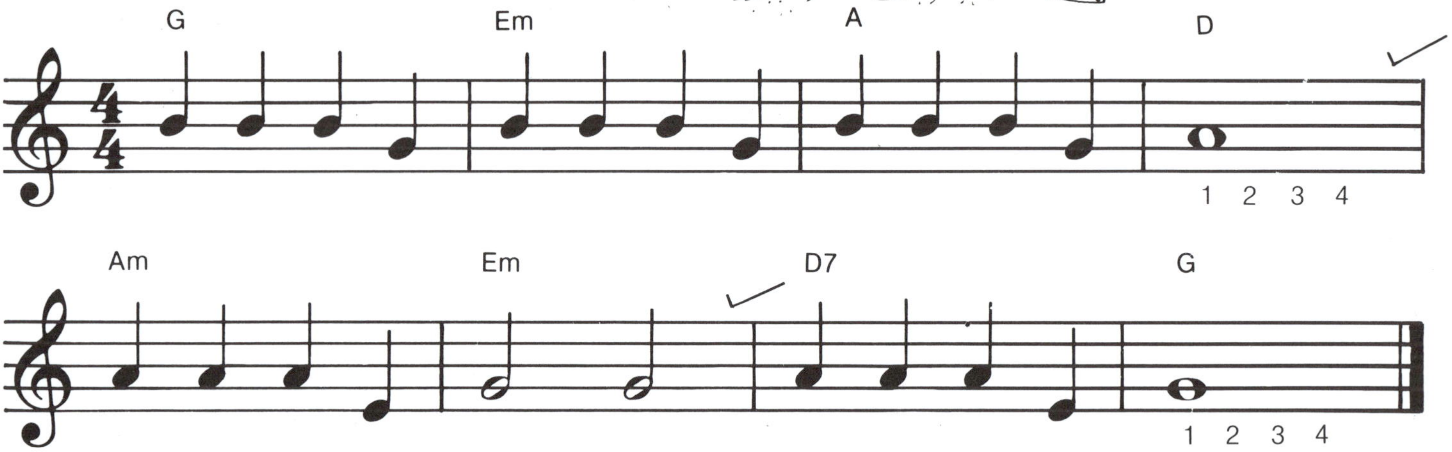

G   Em   A   D

1 2 3 4

Am   Em   D7   G

1 2 3 4

# Harvest Hymn

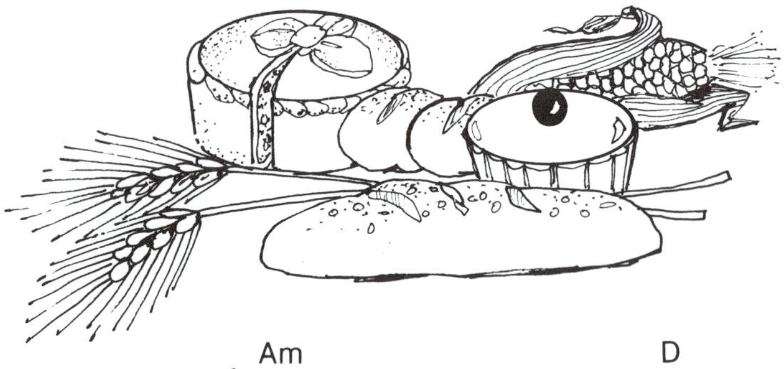

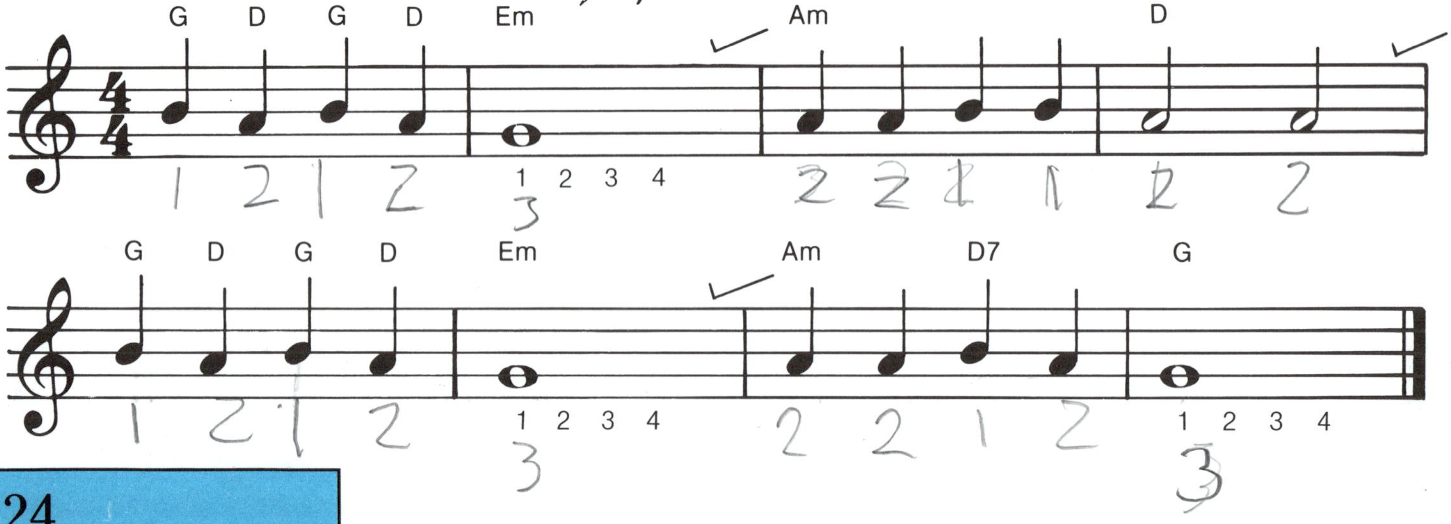

G D G D   Em   Am   D

1 2 1 2   1 2 3 4   2 2 2 1   1 2   2
3

G D G D   Em   Am   D7   G

1 2 1 2   1 2 3 4   2 2 1 2   1 2 3 4
3   3

Here are two songs from **France**.

# Au Clair de la Lune *(In the Moonlight)*

You play the first line; your teacher will play the middle one, and then you play the third line.

**Pupil:**

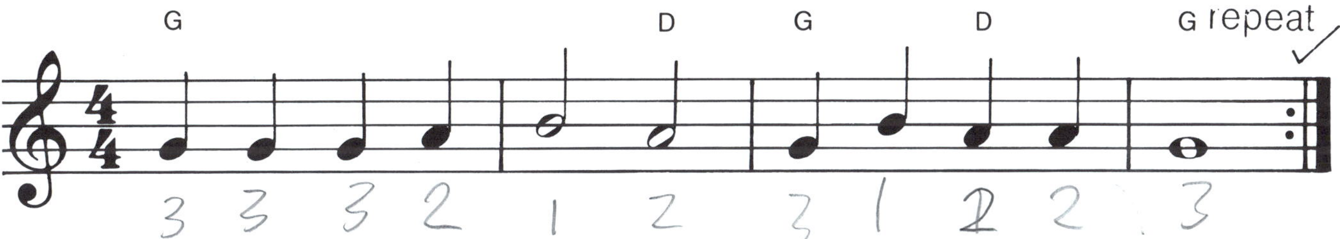


**Teacher:**

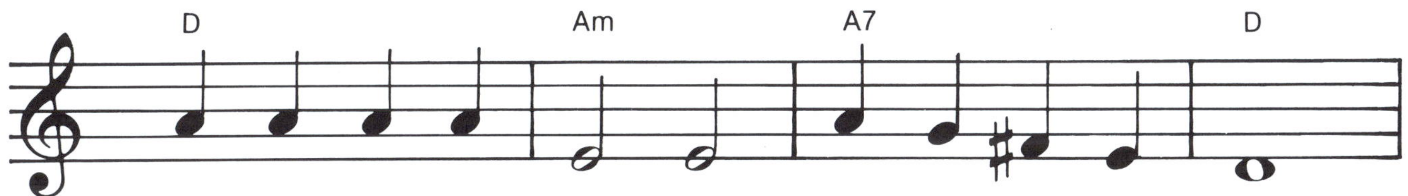


**Pupil:**

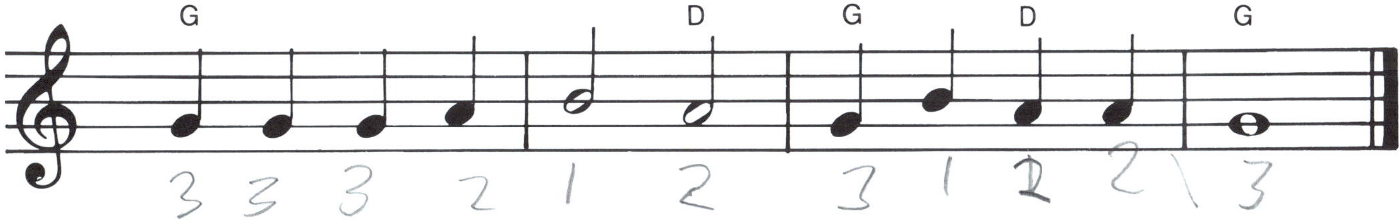


# Lullaby

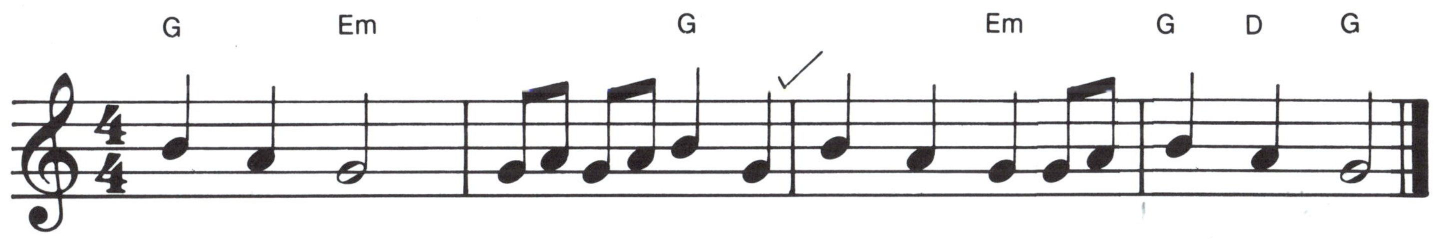

# Crotchet Rest

A **REST** is a silent space in the music. A **CROTCHET REST** means silence for **One** beat.

# Who's that Yonder?

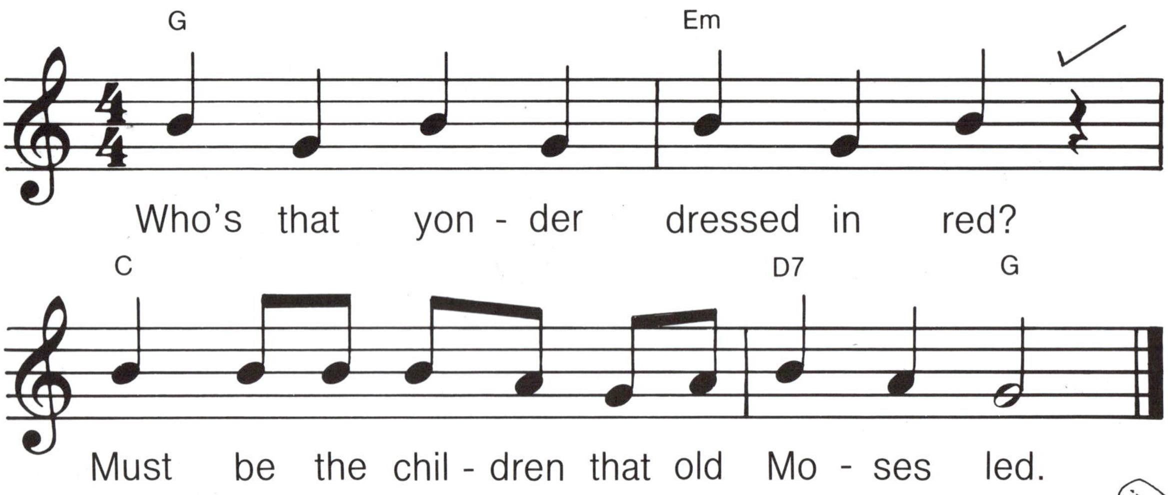

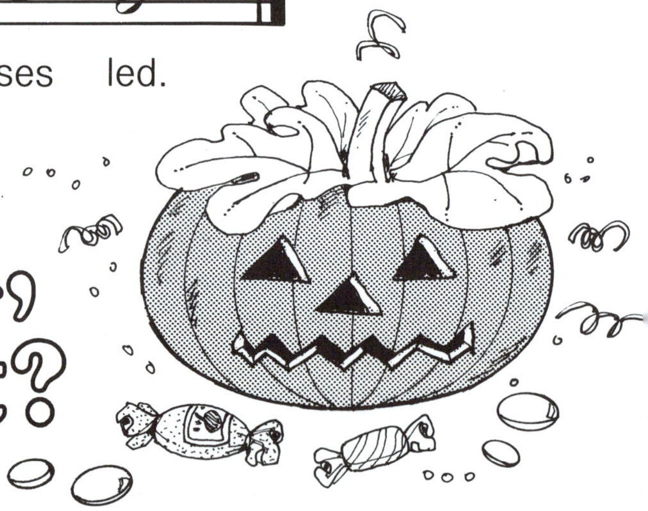

# Knock, Knock, Trick or Treat?

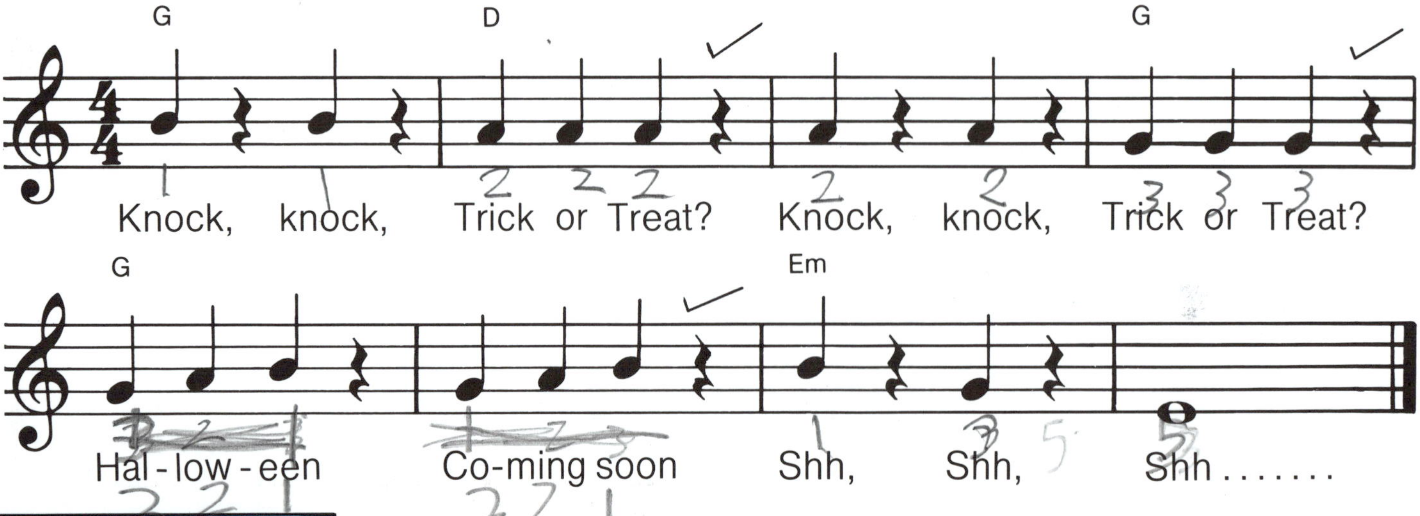

# Dotted Minim

A minim with a dot after it.
It's called a **DOTTED MINIM**, and it's held for **Three** steady beats.

# The Dancing Bear

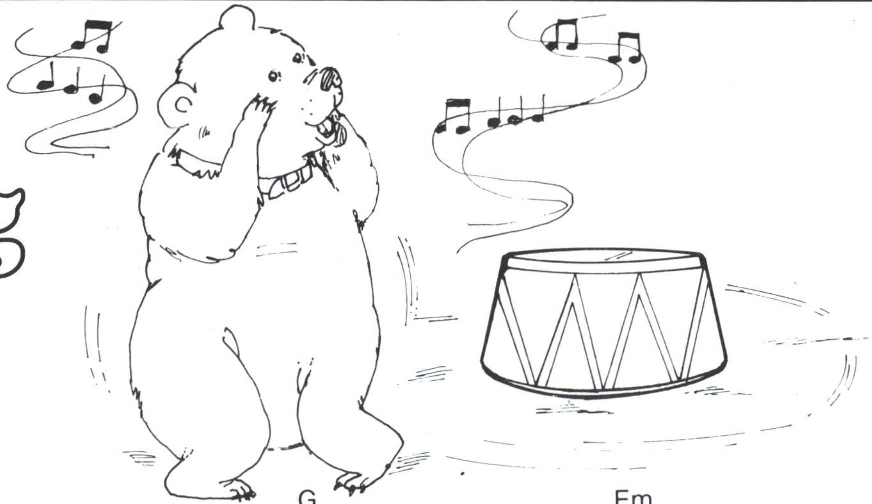

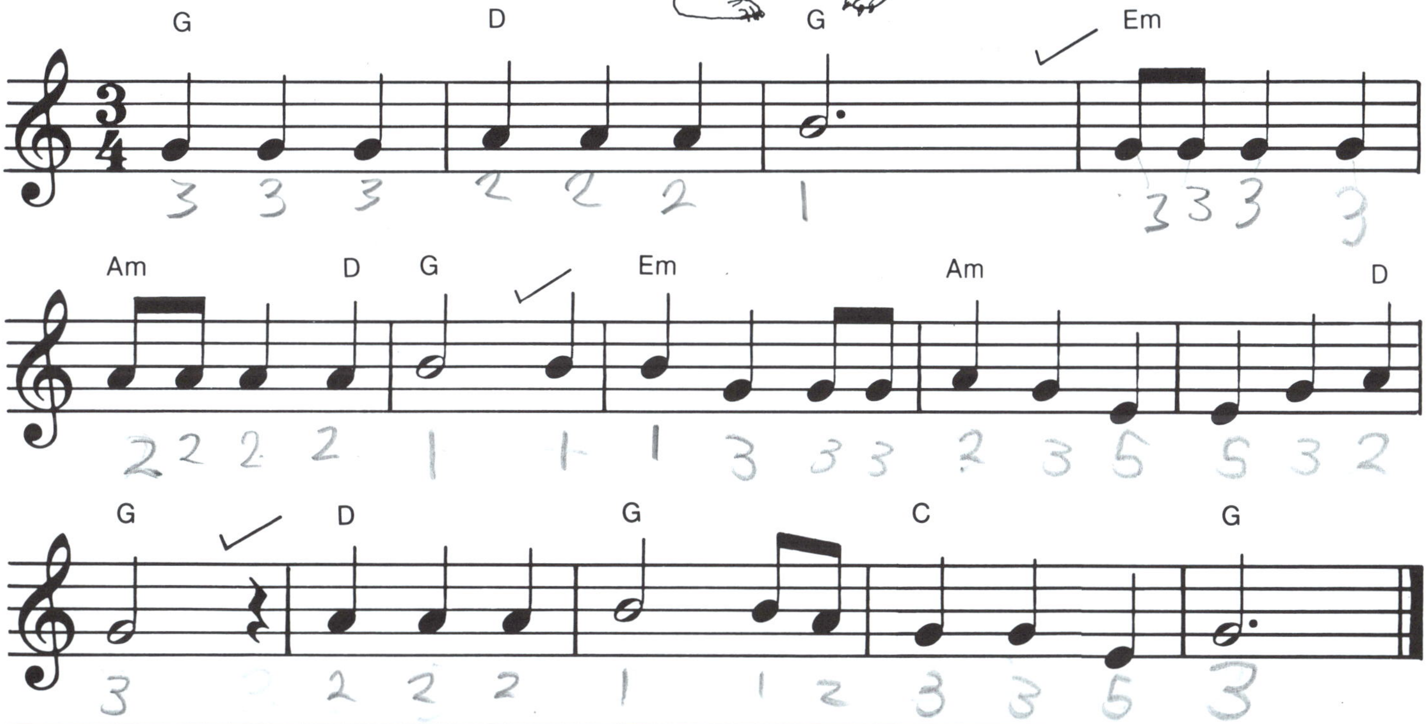

## A New Time Signature

### 3/4

It means there are **Three** crotchet beats (/ / /) in every bar of music.

# Sleepy Bee

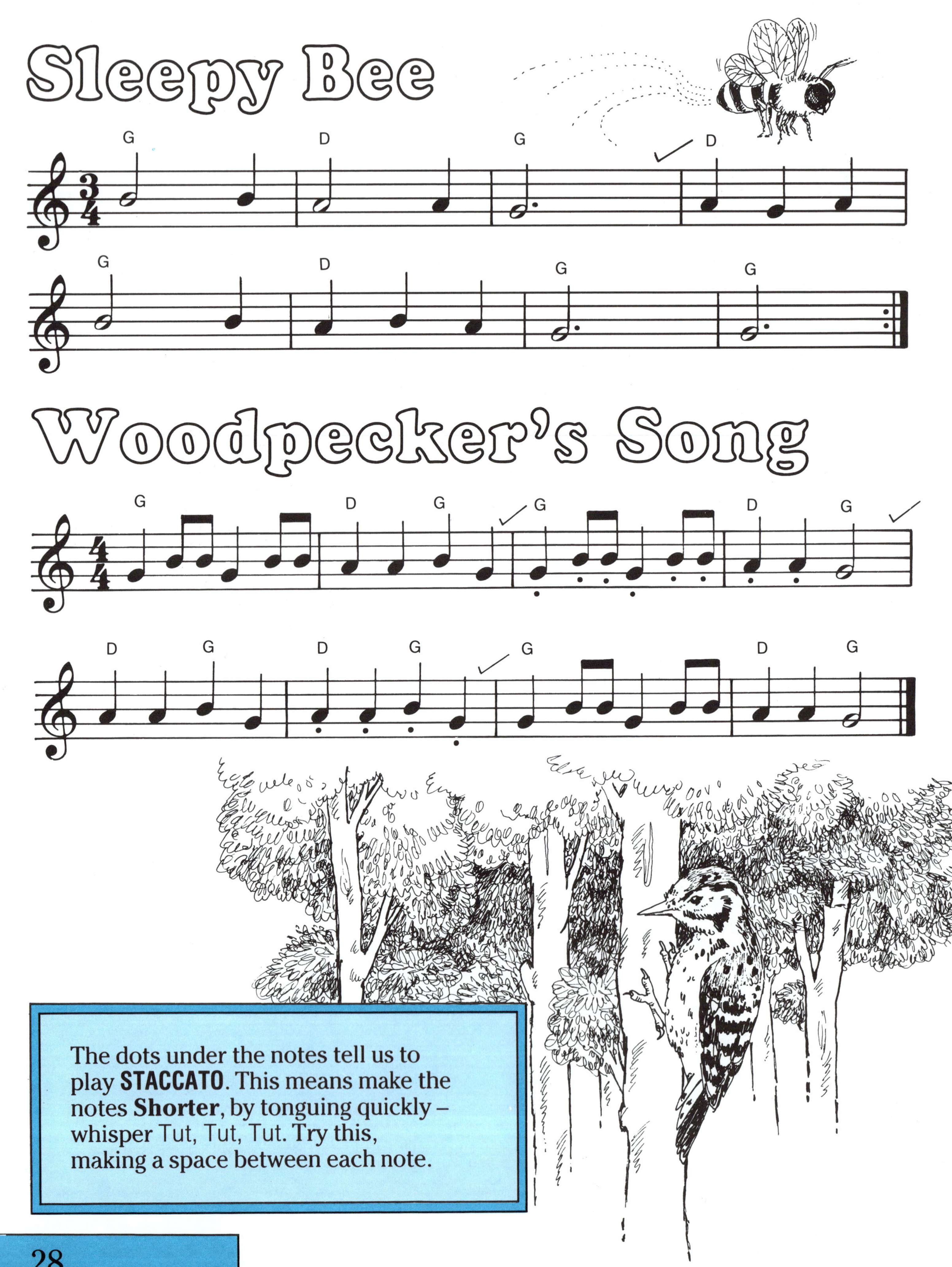

# Woodpecker's Song

# Blowing Games

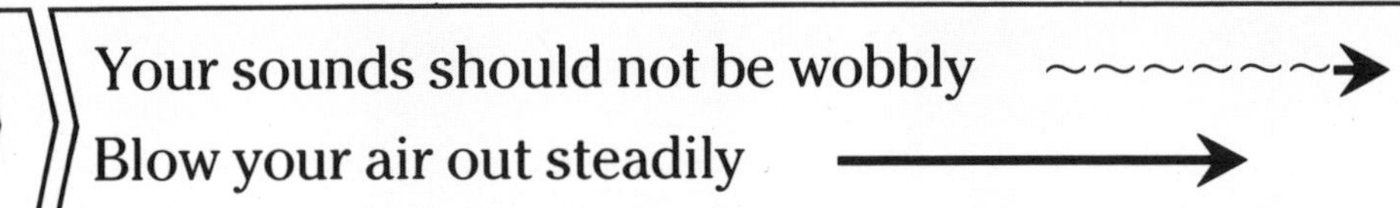



## 1. Does it feel steady?

Hold the palm of your hand up near your mouth. Take a deep breath and blow the air out steadily. **Stop** when the air on your hand feels different. (That's when your breath is not steady.)

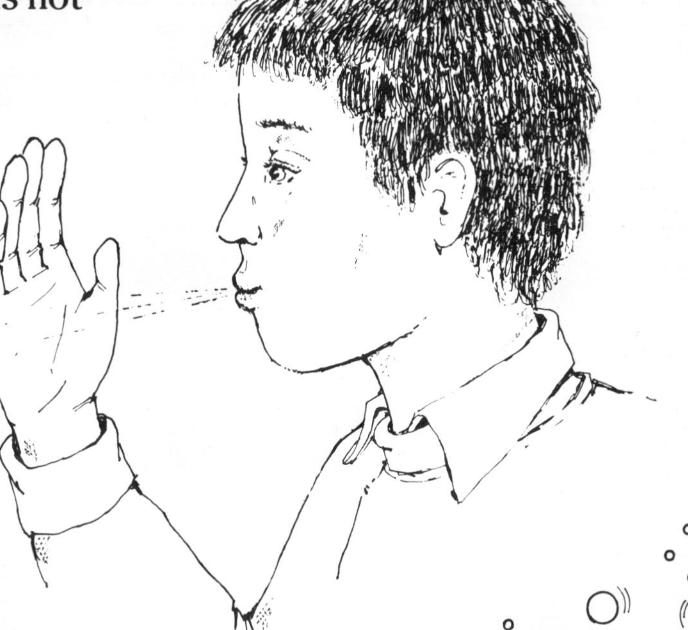

## 2. How long is my steady sound?

Make your chest wide. Take one deep breath, filling out your waistband. Then blow a note steadily, and see how many beats you can hold it for. **Stop** when the note begins to sound wobbly.

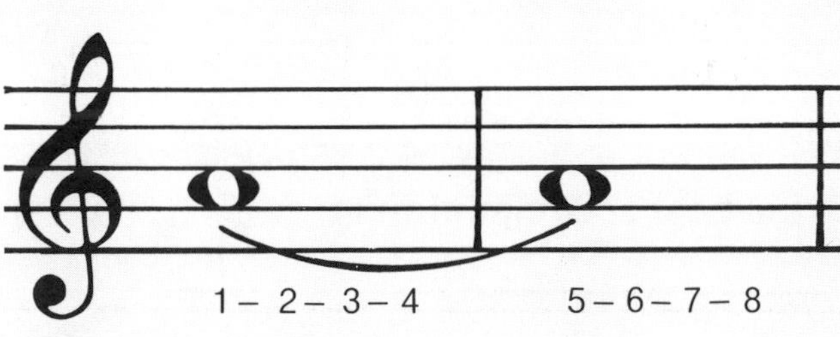

# A Dance Suite on Three Notes

## Waltz

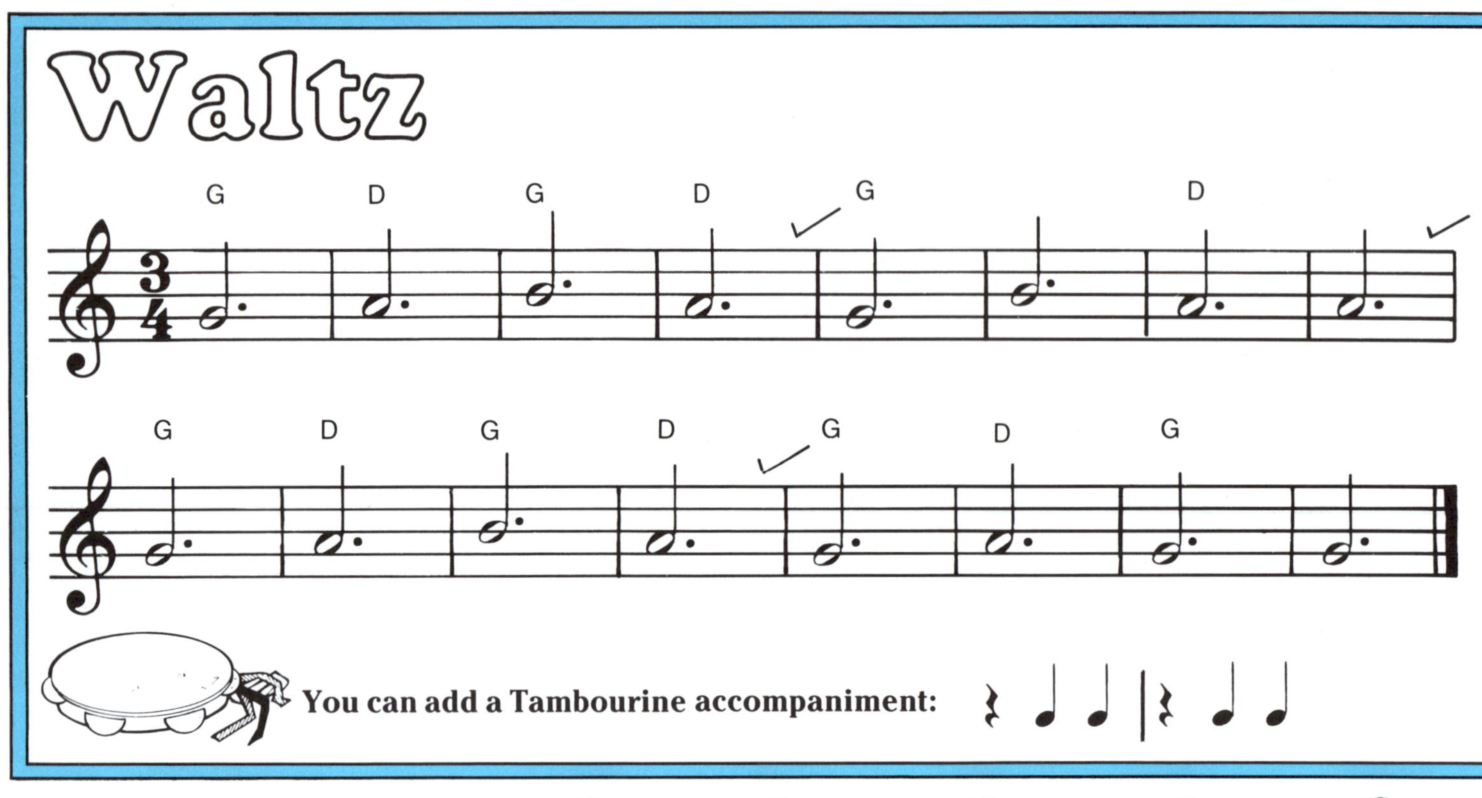

**You can add a Tambourine accompaniment:** 

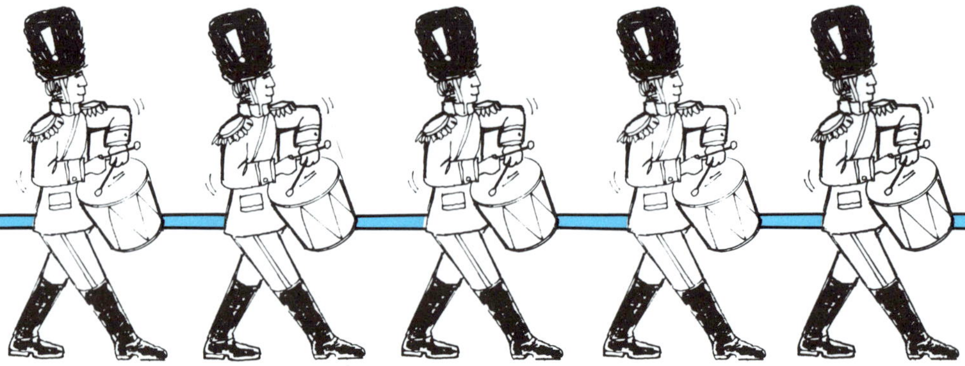

## March

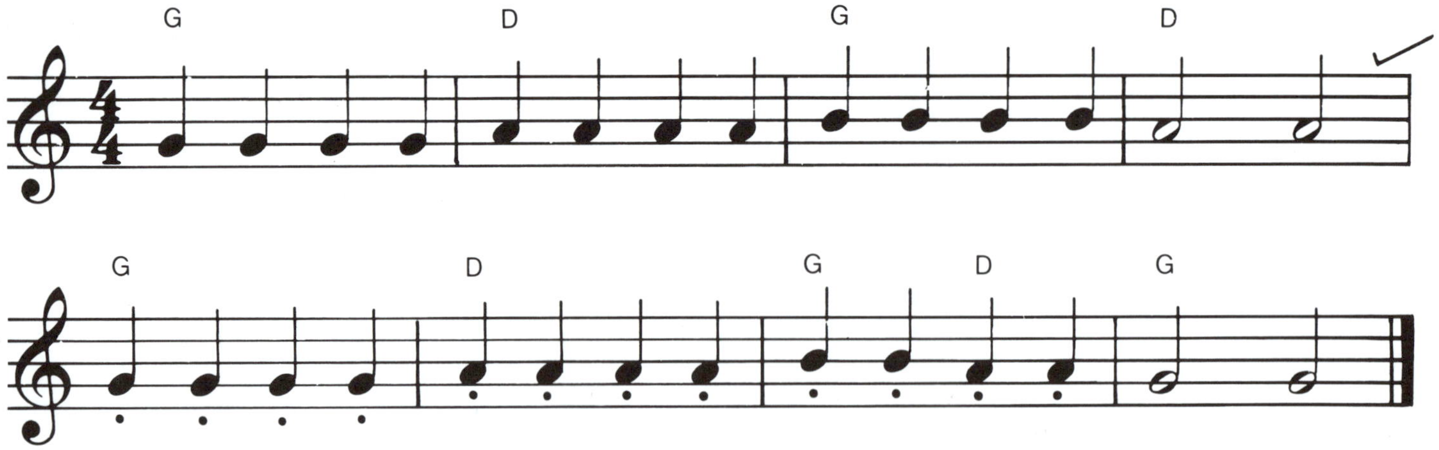

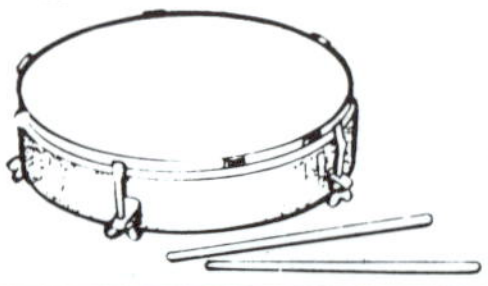

**You can add a Drum beat accompaniment:**

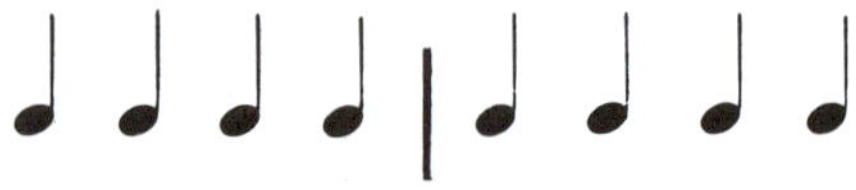

# Polka

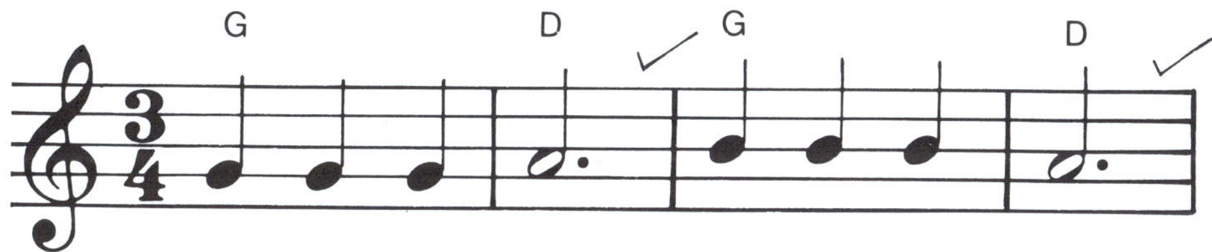

**You can add a Tambourine accompaniment:**

# Minuet

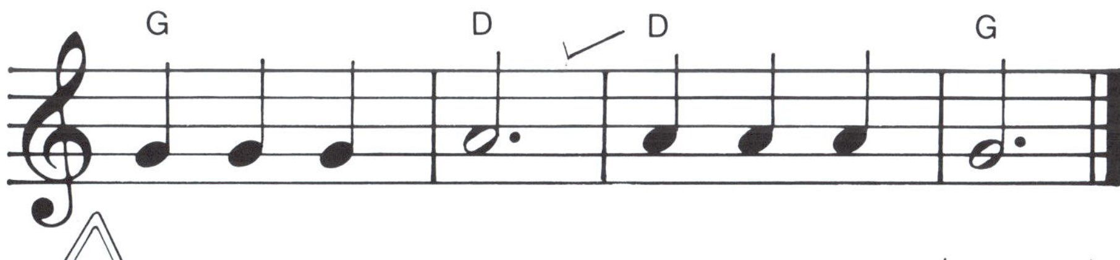


**You can add a Triangle accompaniment:**

A line over a note tells you to play that note a little more strongly.

## How to End a Note Neatly

Push your tongue forward against your top teeth. Keep it there to stop the flow of air. **Try it.**

# Low D

Low D

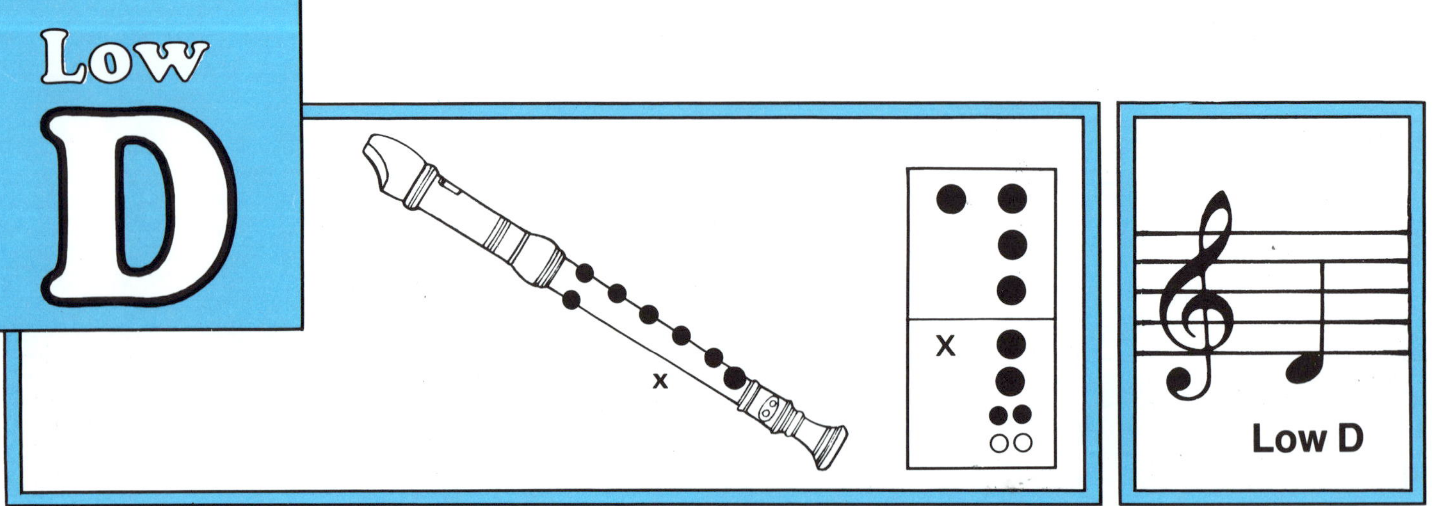

Our next note is **Low D.**

Start from **HOME BASE** (E). Then add right hand finger 3.

# Old Macdonald had a Farm

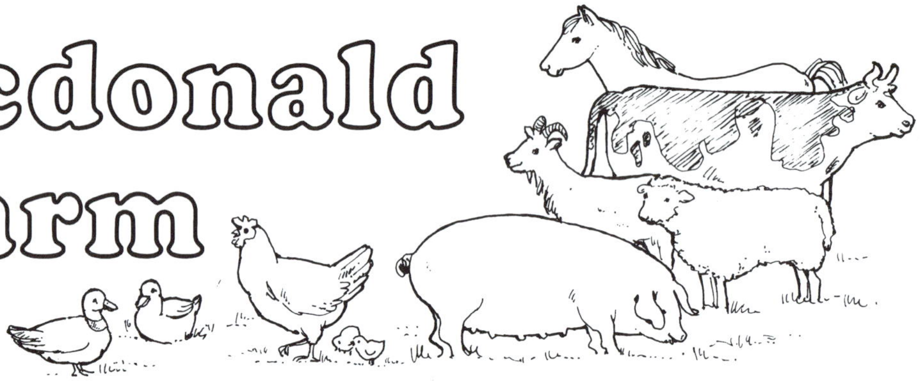

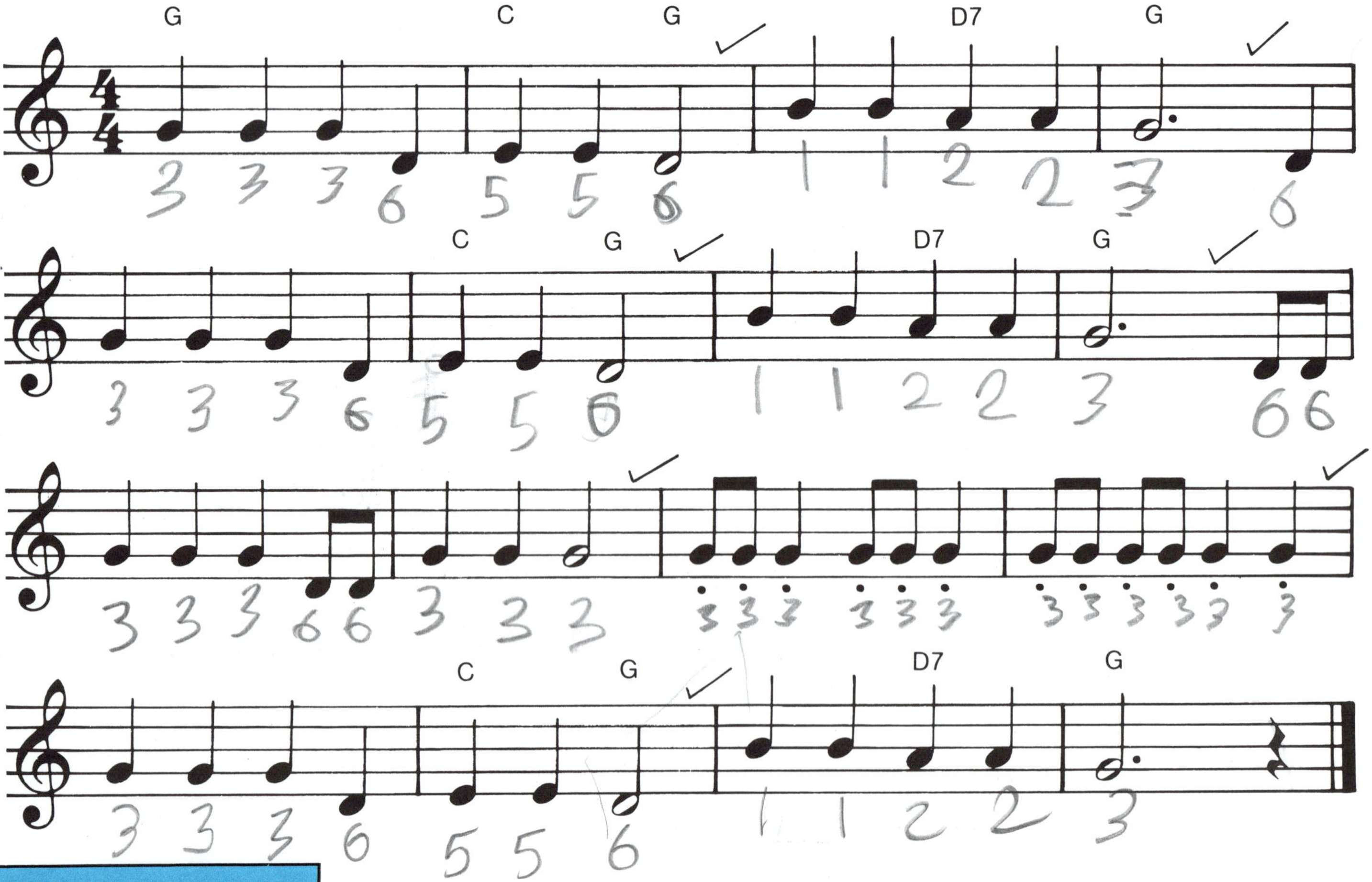

# Chopsticks

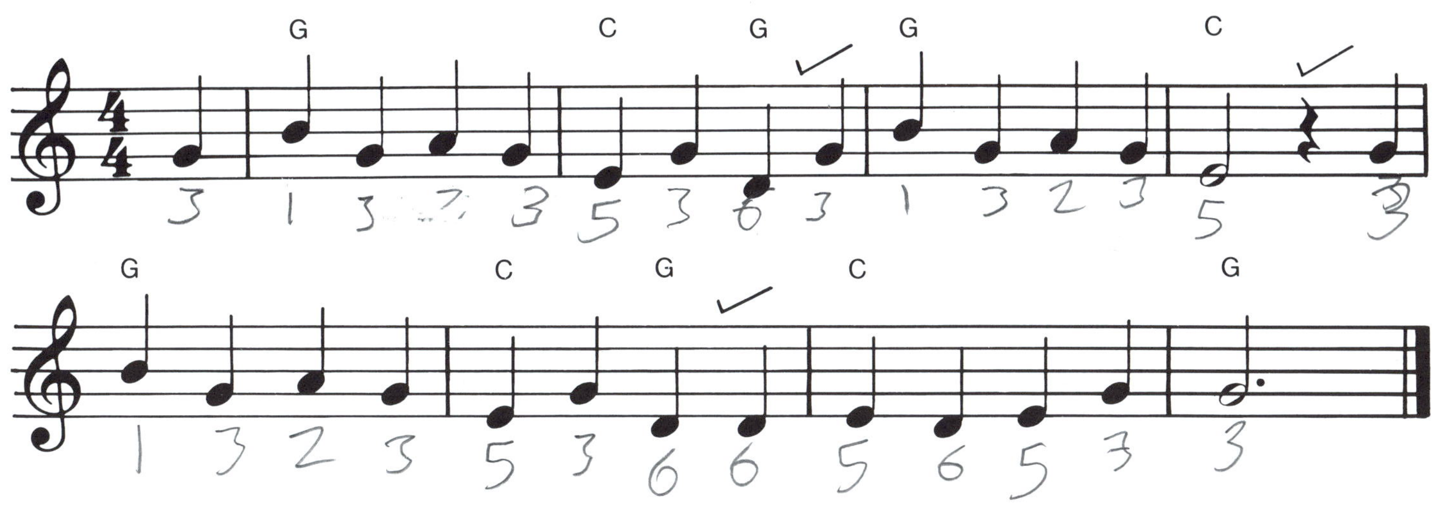


# It's Me, oh Lord

Not all tunes begin on the first beat of a bar. The tunes on this page begin just before the barline – on the **UPBEAT.** Play the upbeat lightly.

# Big Ben

# Trumpet Fanfare

**(by Kim, aged 9)**

# French Hunting Song

# The Slur

The **SLUR** is a curved line joining notes that are **different**, like this.

It tells us to make the notes glide **smoothly**, without a break.

# How to Slur

Tongue only the **first note**. Then keep your tongue **still** while you play the joined notes in **one long breath**.

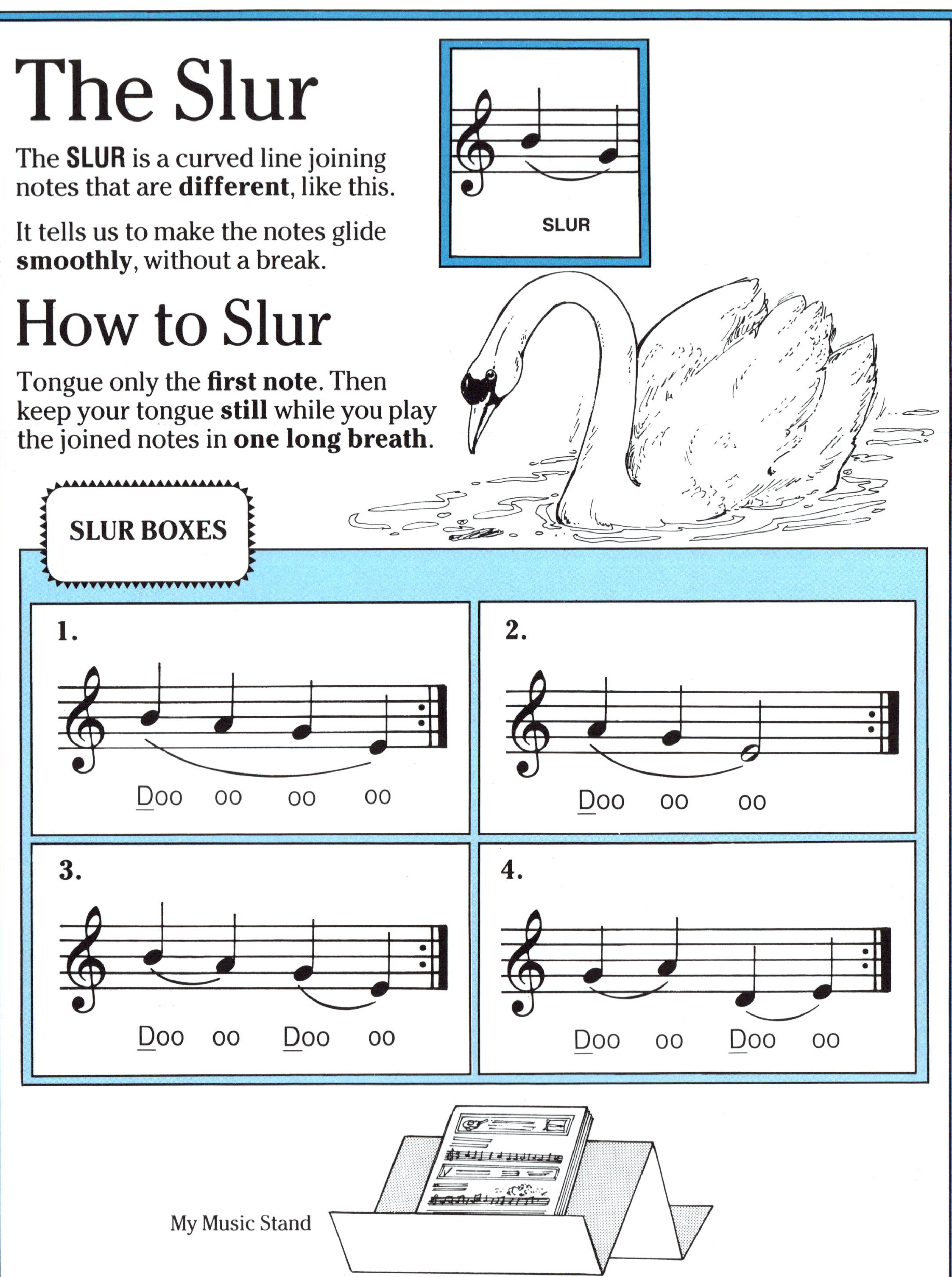

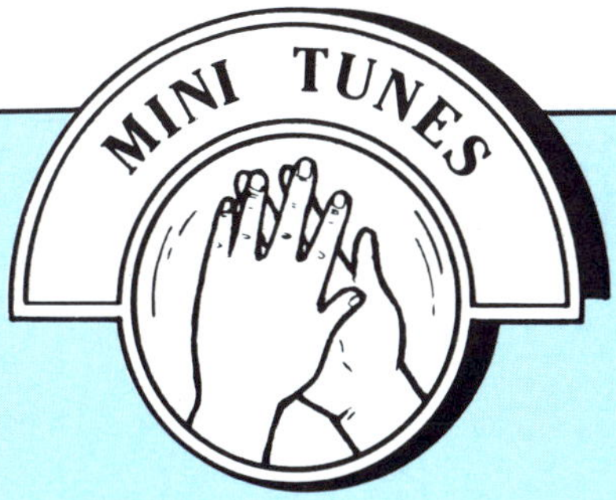

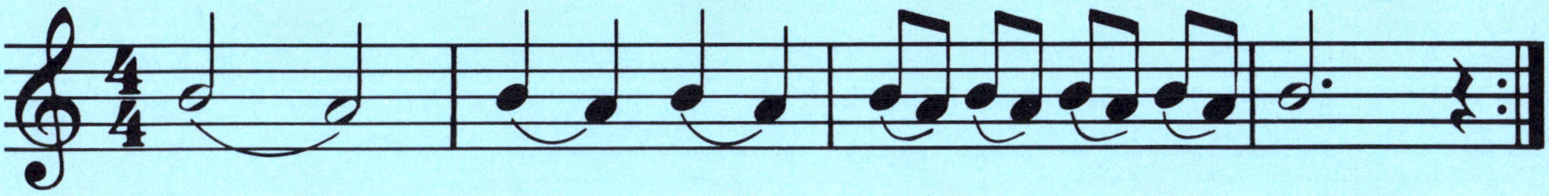

# There's a Hole in my Bucket

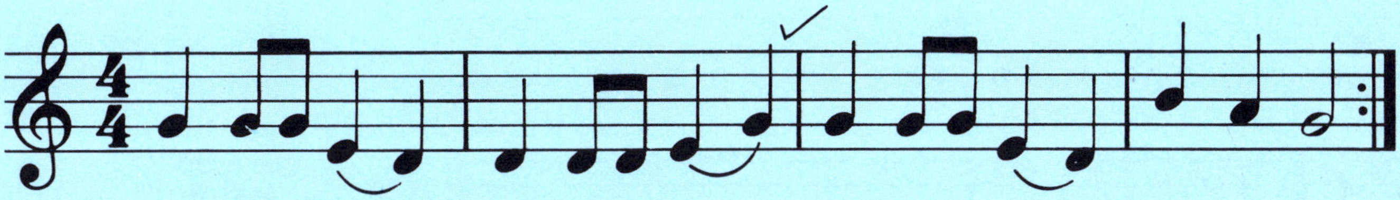

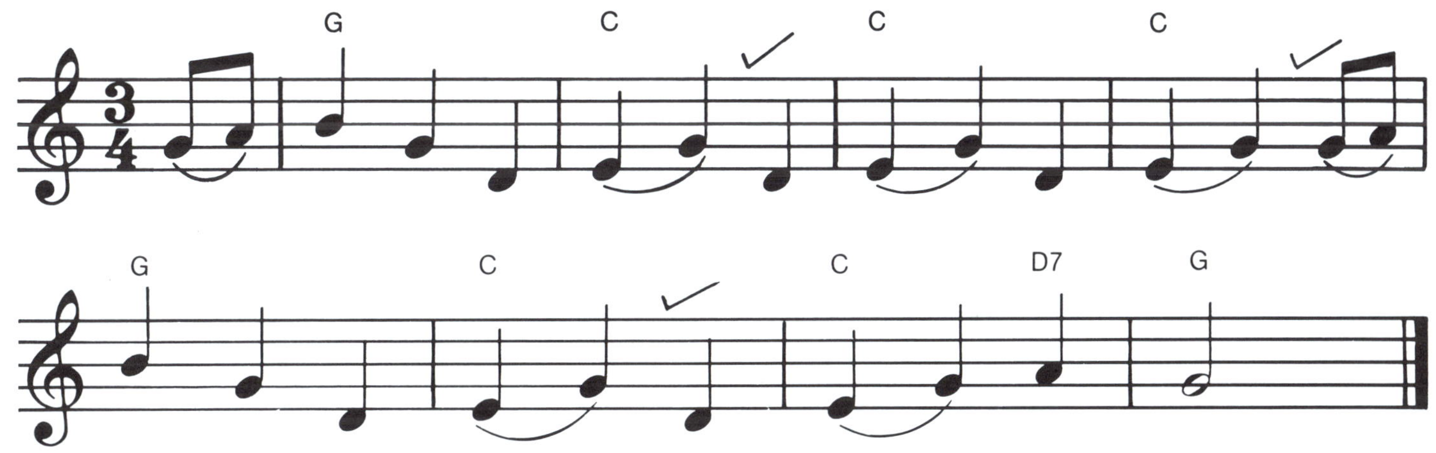

**Make sure you can play SLURS before you go on.**

# Wayfaring Stranger

# Sleep, Baby, Sleep

Now play **'Sleep, Baby, Sleep'** again **without** the **SLURS**, tonguing every note. Which way do you prefer?

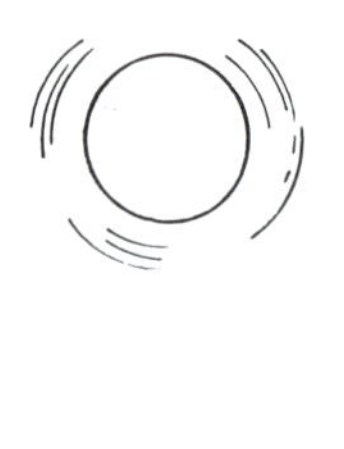

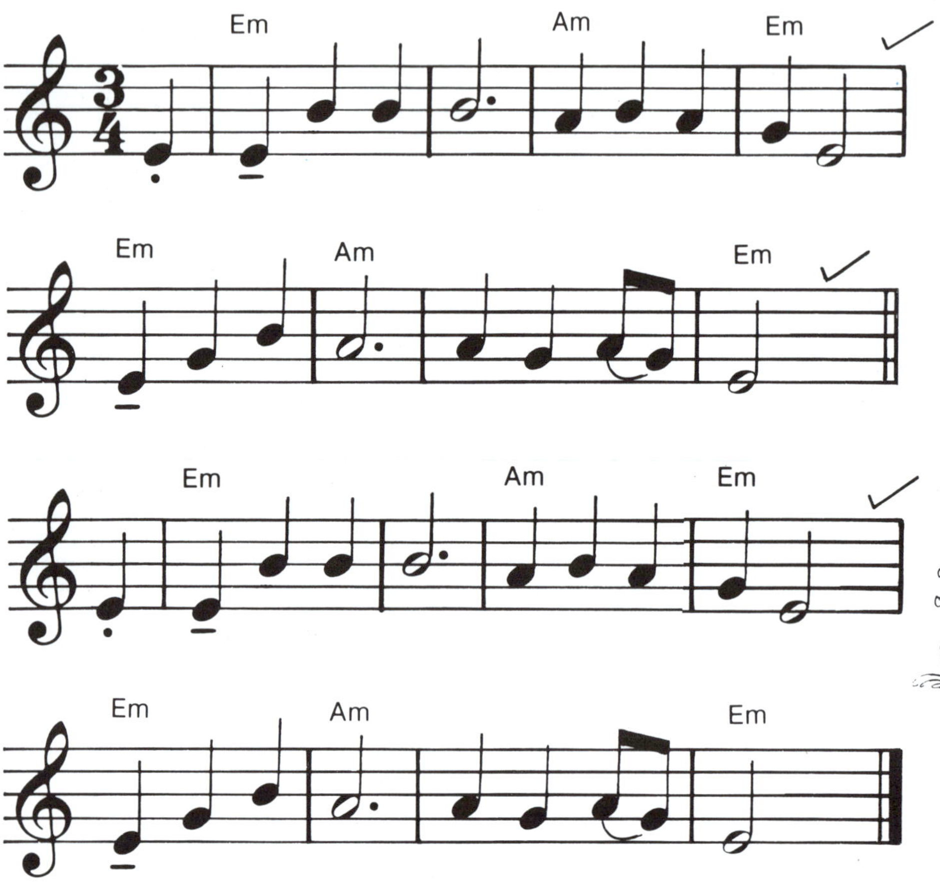

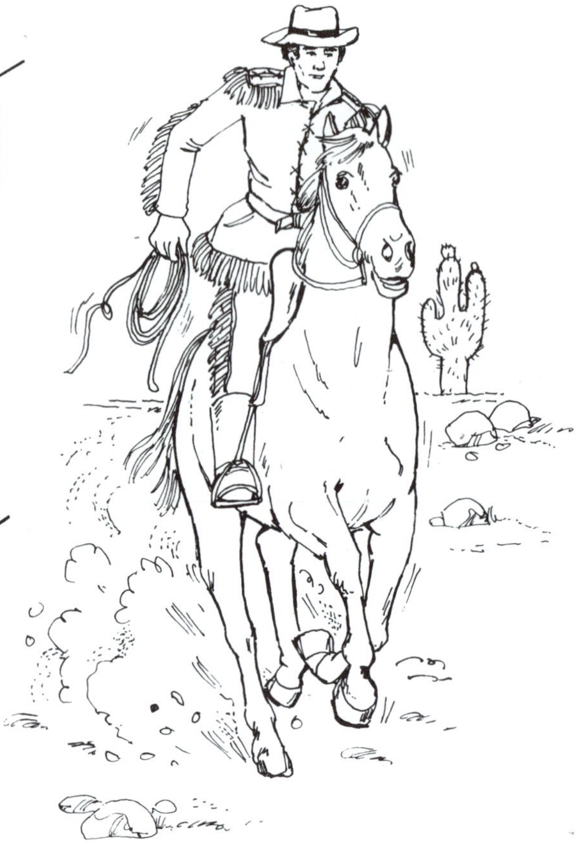

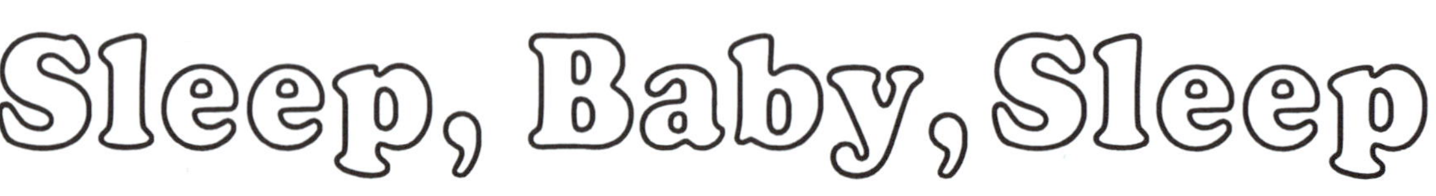

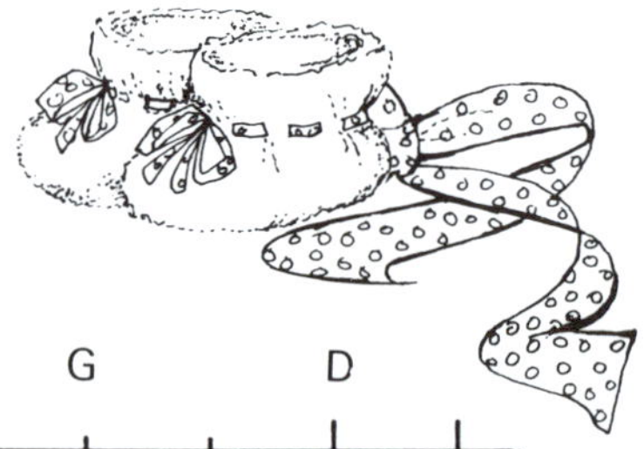

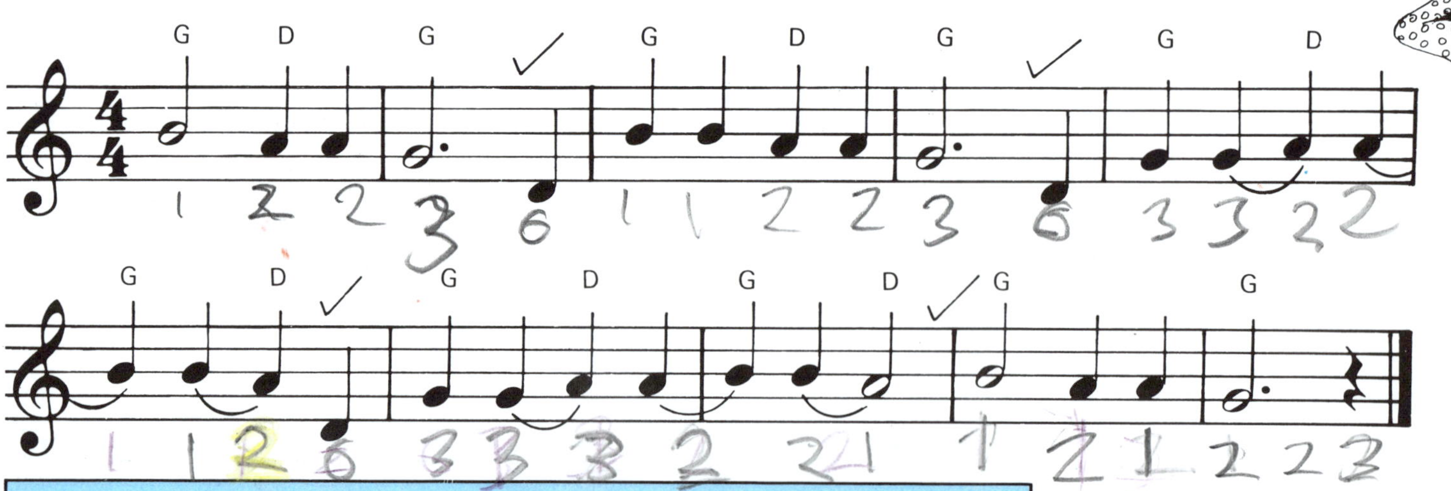

Jolly Old St. Nicholas

G          D7              Em              Bm
Jol - ly old St.   Ni - cho - las,   Lean your ear this way!
When the clock is   stri-king twelve,   When I'm fast a - sleep,

C              G              Am      A        D
Don't you tell a   sin - gle soul   What I'm going to say.
Down the chim-ney,   broad and black,   With your pack you'll creep.

G          D7              Em              Bm
Christ-mas Eve is   com - ing fast,   Now, you dear old man,
All the stock-ings   you will find   Hang - ing in a row.

C              G              Am      D7       G
Whis-per what you'll   bring to me,   Tell me if you can.
Mine will be the   short - est one,   You'll be sure to know.

39

# Index of Tunes



# Some New Notes
# Ready for Part 2

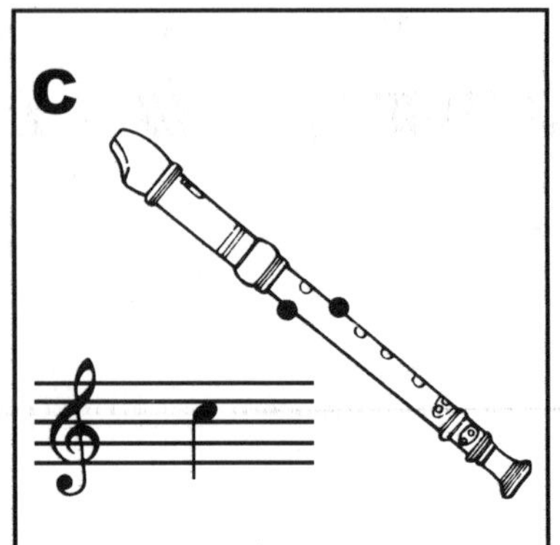


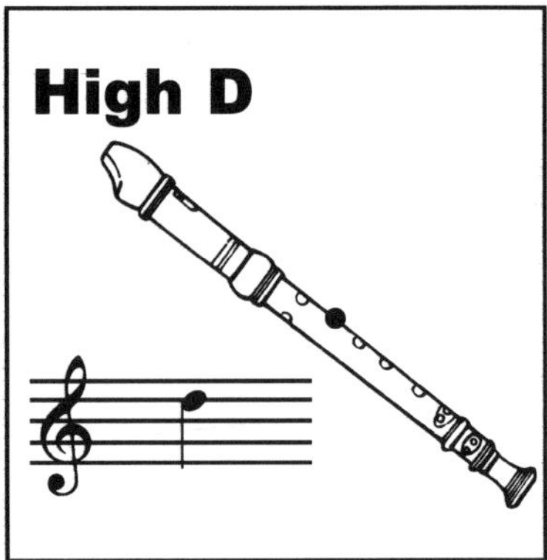

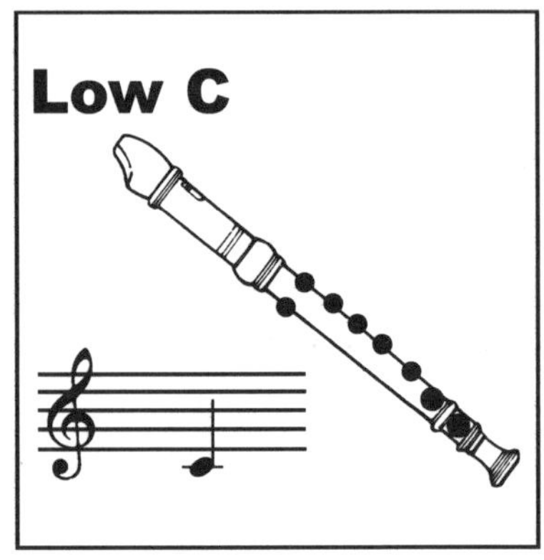